PUBLICATIONS ON THE NEAR EAST
UNIVERSITY OF WASHINGTON
NUMBER 3

Sohráb Gains the Upper Hand: The Second Day from the
Houghton *Shahname*, folio 153v (private collection).

The Tragedy of Sohráb and Rostám

from the Persian National Epic,
the Shahname of Abol-Qasem Ferdowsi

REVISED EDITION

Translated by Jerome W. Clinton

UNIVERSITY OF WASHINGTON PRESS
SEATTLE • LONDON

Sponsored by
the Department of
Near Eastern Languages and Civilization
and the
Middle East Center
of the Henry M. Jackson School
of International Studies
University of Washington

Cover: Detail of *Sohráb Gains the Upper Hand:*
The Second Day from the Houghton *Shahname,*
folio 153v (private collection)

University of Washington Press
PO Box 50096
Seattle, WA 98145-5096, U.S.A.
www.washington.edu/uwpress

Library of Congress Cataloging-in-Publication Data

Firdawsī.
[Rustam va Suhrāb. English and Persian]
The tragedy of Sohráb and Rostám:
from the Persian national epic, the Shahname of
Abol-Qasem Ferdowski / translated by Jerome W. Clinton.—Rev. ed.
p. cm.—(Publications on the Near East, University of Washington; 3)
Persian text with parallel English translation.
Includes bibliographical references.
ISBN 0-295-97567-9 (alk. paper)
I. Clinton, Jerome W. II. Title. III. Series.
PK6456.A12R82   1996
891'.5511—dc20   96-19208

This book has received grants in aid of publication from

The Persian Heritage Foundation
Princeton University

For Julia, Matthew, and Gabriella

Contents

Acknowledgments

This translation has had a long gestation. I began it in 1980 out of a sense of frustration with existing translations. They had kept pace neither with the editions of the text, nor with modern English. I worked at it intermittently for several years, picking it up and putting it down many times as other work intruded. Then in the spring of 1985, I had several months free and decided that I should finish it. It took me six months rather than the three I had anticipated. The longer I worked the clearer it became that the tragedy of Rostám and Sohráb deserved something better than the academic prose I had had in mind when I started, and so I retranslated the whole of it.

A number of people have helped me along the way. Some by emphasizing the virtues of what I had done, others by pointing out its limitations. I would like in particular to thank Walter Andrews, Jere L. Bacharach, Nahoma Clinton, Walter Feldman, James Haba, and Roy P. Mottahedeh.

Princeton University's Office of Research and Project Administration provided me with computer time and equipment over several years. I am happy to acknowledge their patient and generous support here.

Finally, I would like to thank my editor, Felicia J. Hecker, for her enthusiasm, patience, and speed. I thought such editors existed only in authors' dreams.

Introduction

The story of Sohráb is just one small portion of the vast compilation of stories that make up the Iranian national epic commonly known as the *Shahname*, or Book of Kings. The *Shahname* traces the history of the Iranian nation from the first mythological shah, Kiumars, down to the defeat and death of the last Sassanian emperor, Yazdegerd III, at the hands of the Arab armies of Islam in the middle of the seventh century A.D.

The events narrated in the first two-thirds of the *Shahname*, tales both heroic and romantic, belong to a mythical or legendary time. In the last third, these events are set in historical times, and stories are introduced from the biography of Alexander the Great and from the history of the Parthian and Sassanian dynasties (247 B.C.–A.D. 651). But the style of presentation does not change. Historical figures and events are presented as the stuff of myth and legend.

The *Shahname* does not begin as Homeric epics do "in the midst of things," but with the appearance of the first shah, Kiumars. Mankind seems to have existed before him, but as an undifferentiated species. The formation of human society required the shaping presence of a shah. And other shahs, most notably Jamshid, the Iranian Solomon, provide human society with those things—fire, tools, agriculture, and the various crafts—that raise men and women above the level of beasts. The history of the Iranian nation from that point on assumes the existence of a divinely chosen ruler. Indeed, while there are a number of recurrent themes in the *Shahname*, such as the immortality of noble deeds, the malignancy of fate, and its inevitability, and the persistent hostility and envy of Iran's neighbors, the theme that underlies all of these is that God prefers Iran to other nations, and sustains it through the institution of monarchy. So long as there is a shah, there will be an Iran. When Yazdegerd III is slain in A.D. 652, the Iran of the *Shahname* comes to an end.

As the continuous thread that holds this vast compilation together is dynastic succession, so the principal figures that people its tales are Iran's shahs and the members of their court. Like Malory's *Le Morte d'Arthur*, its focus is that of the court and its concerns to the exclusion of the world outside. War and feasting, hunting and feats of strength and skill, courtly intrigue and struggles for succession to the throne are the events and themes of its narratives. Moreover, these same subjects are the sources of incident and imagery as well, not the everyday concerns of farmers, herdsmen, artisans or traders, nor the details of domestic life. Each day dawns with the sun as an invincible warrior advancing over the mountains to put the armies of night to flight with his shining blade. The coming of spring is seen in the palace garden where the blossoming flowers are described as precious gems or rich brocade. Armies on the move seem to pass through a landscape devoid of life and character until they encounter the goal of their march—another army, a fortress, a fortified city.

Although the Divinity's support for Iranian monarchy is a central constant of the *Shahname*, its ideology is not a naïve and enthusiastic monarchism. Abol-Qasem Ferdowsi (d. ca. 1025), who gave the *Shahname* its present form, was not a panegyrist who presented idealizations of the ruler for the admiration of royal sponsors and their followers. He was as realistic about the limitations of individual monarchs as was Shakespeare. Many of the greatest tales in the epic are as much concerned with the dilemmas of the monarchial state as they are its inevitability. In the story translated here, for example, Sohráb must be killed, even though he is Rostám's son, because he has sworn to overthrow Shah Kavús and set his father on the throne. This violates both the sanctity of the shah and the principle of divine selection. And the reason that Rostám, Iran's foremost hero, must be the one who kills his son is that he has been slack in his loyalty to the shah, albeit with good reason. He has repeatedly saved the shah from the consequences of his rash and foolish actions. Still, Kavús remains remarkably ungrateful and even threatens Rostám's life when he is slow to respond to the shah's summons. But in the end, both familial bonds and personal dignity must be sacrificed to instant and unwavering obedience to even so unworthy a shah as Kavús.

In the next tale, Kavús places his own son, Siyavosh, in the untenable position of having to choose between obeying his father or honoring an oath taken before God. When Siyavosh chooses the latter, he, too, is destroyed. Kavús, who by his action has deprived Iran of a loyal and exemplary prince and condemned his country to a protracted conflict with Turán, escapes punishment completely. As the prologue to the story of Sohráb says, the ways of the Creator are mysterious, God exacts a high price for his support of the Iranian nation.

The History of the Shahname

It is virtually impossible to put a date to the origins of a national epic tradition. Yet one can say with confidence that many of the stories that make up the *Shahname* are of great, if undetermined, antiquity. Herodotus tells us that in the time of Darius, the accounts of Iran's kings and heroes were celebrated in story and song. And many of the characters and events that appear in the *Shahname* appear as well in the Zoroastrian scripture, the Avesta, which dates from the time of Cyrus and Darius, some 2,500 years ago. We also know that this national epic tradition was an active and vital one, and that stories from it circulated widely in several languages and in a number of versions. From time to time monarchs sponsored recensions of these stories that attempted to bring together the versions of the various stories that had become current in different parts of the vast Iranian empire. We know of one such recension that was prepared at the behest of the Sassanian monarch Khosrow Anushirvan in the mid sixth century A.D. Another dates from just after the accession of Yazdegerd III in the mid seventh century. However, while these versions may be said to have had official sanction, none became the sole and authoritative text. On the contrary, it is clear that the stories were transmitted both orally and in writing, in prose and poetry, and in several languages down to the late tenth century, when the greatest poet of the national epic, Abol-Qasem Ferdowsi, undertook the task of producing a new and comprehensive poetic rendering of the whole work.

Ferdowsi was able to draw upon a wide variety of sources. The Sassanian recension was surely one of them, but probably in an Arabic translation, or, rather, in a variety of translations. The Iranian epic materials were rendered into Arabic by many scholars and in many ways after the Islamic conquest of the seventh century. Ferdowsi also seems to have had access to an extensive store of oral material, to a prose recension in the Persian of his day, and, possibly, to untranslated Middle Persian texts. These sources have now largely vanished, in part because of the success of Ferdowsi's work.

During the thirty-five years that he devoted to this task, Ferdowsi was as much a scholar and editor as he was a poet and author. He not only gave the *Shahname* what was to become its definitive poetic form, he also determined which stories from among the many that made up the tradition would be included, and in which versions. In the first few decades after the Ferdowsian recension of the *Shahname* began to circulate, other poets gave poetic form to chapters of the national epic that they felt he had slighted—perhaps motivated as much by a desire to imitate his success as to "correct" his version—but these never came to enjoy the currency of his work, and many are known to us only by name.[1]

In the *Shahname*, Ferdowsi at times speaks of his own role as that of one who has given new life to tales that had long fallen into oblivion: "These stories, long grown old, will be renewed / By me, and men will tell them everywhere" (3:6:9).[2] And he clearly thought of himself as a reviver of a tradition that had come to be disregarded. The reason for this decline of the national tradition is the Arab conquest of the seventh century, and the subsequent spread of Islam. The national epic was so deeply identified with the royal court that when that court was overthrown and Iran's shahs were replaced by rulers who spoke a different language, had entirely different cultural traditions, and were militant advocates of an entirely new religion, the decline of the *Shahname* was an inevitable consequence. Ferdowsi alludes to this profound cultural transformation brought about by the spread of Islam to Iran and its effects upon the Iranian tradition in a famous passage toward the close of the poem. The commander of the Iranian army, who was decisively defeated by the Arab forces at Qadesiya, reads Iran's fortunes in the stars and predicts both the coming defeat of his army and the ultimate decline of the Iranian nation:

> They'll set the *minbar* level with the throne,
> And name their children Omar and Osman.
> Then will our heavy labors come to ruin.
> Oh, from this height a long descent begins.
> You'll see no throne or court or diadem;
> The stars will smile upon the Arab host.
> And after many days a time will come
> When one unworthy wears the royal robes.
> . . . .
> Then men will break their compact with the truth
> And crookedness and lies will be held dear.
> (9:318:88–91, 97)

The Iranian tradition declined for nearly two centuries until Iranian dynasties, beginning with the Samanids in the late ninth century, once more gained ascendancy over Central Asia and the Iranian plateau, land that had traditionally been the heart of Iran's empire. Although they were now themselves Muslims, and Arabic had permeated their language and culture, they made the revival of Persian poetry and the Iranian national epic a conscious policy. The Samanids, like Iranian monarchs before them, sponsored the preparation of a comprehensive prose recension of the text, and encouraged an eminent poet of the time, Daqiqi (d. ca. 980), to turn it into poetry. When he died before the task was completed, or even well begun, it fell to Ferdowsi to finish the work. In the process, he revived the stories of the *Shahname* and made them current. For this reason, Ferdowsi is revered in Iran as much for his service to Iranian culture as for his genius as a poet. His reward was that immortality of reputation that he had so accurately predicted:

> And when this famous book shall reach its end,
> Throughout the land my praises will be heard.
> From that day on I shall not die, but live,
> For I'll have sown my words both far and wide.
>   (9:382:863–64)

The Shahname *after Ferdowsi*

The development of the text of the *Shahname* does not stop with Ferdowsi, however, for it was never seen as a sacred book that must be preserved with immaculate textual exactitude. Our earliest manuscript of the *Shahname* was discovered recently in Florence—where it had been miscatalogued as a Koran commentary—and dates from 1216, two centuries after Ferdowsi completed his work. It is the first volume of a two-volume set, and contains only the first half of the text's 50,000 couplets. The next oldest manuscript, and the first to contain the complete text, is that of the British.Museum, which was copied in 1276. The British Museum manuscript served as the basis for the only attempt in modern times to make a critical edition, that of the Soviet Academy of Sciences, which was begun in 1960 and completed eleven years later. As close as the British Museum manuscript is to the Florence manuscript, it differs from it in ways that cannot simply be explained as scribal error. The choice of words in individual lines frequently differs between the two manuscripts, each has numerous lines not found in the other, and the sequence of incidents in stories may also vary. In short, it appears that even at this early date the text had begun to be affected by other versions of the stories and the personalities of the scribes and poets who transmitted it.

From the fourteenth century on, many manuscripts, some clearly identified as recensions, not simple copies, and all somewhat fuller than their predecessors, were produced. To give only one example of how the text has grown, Sohráb's tale, which contains 1,050 couplets in the earliest manuscripts, has grown to 1,459 couplets in the nineteenth-century manuscript edited by Jules Mohl, from which both his own translation into French was made, and that of Arthur George and Edmond Warner's into English. The changes most often amplify the story rather than alter events or characterization, but sometimes they seem to have been made with the intention of adapting a story to the expectations of its audience. In later versions of the tale, Tahminé and Rostám are given a proper, Islamic-style wedding, for instance, not simply allowed to co-habit as mutually consenting adults.

The tales are also recited and elaborated upon in Iranian coffeehouses, and there are, in addition, popular, oral versions that circulate widely, and that often contain startling differences from the manuscript versions of the text. Sohráb becomes a daughter in one, and in another he is not slain at all. The *Shahname* tradition, in short, is still one of continuing currency and vitality.

The Cultural Importance of the Shahname

The *Shahname* has had a sustained and vital influence within its cultural tradition comparable to that of the Old Testament or Homer's works within theirs. It depicts the beliefs and values of Iranian society as they were before the coming of Islam, and so has helped to mark them as distinctive within the complex mix of elements that make up Islamic culture. Its heroes embody ideals of personal conduct that are still current, and its vision of Iranian society as one that is sustained by a divinely sanctioned monarchy pervades the whole course of Iranian history. For nearly a thousand years, the *Shahname* has also served poets and historians as a source of illustrative incident, a reference grammar of narrative technique, and a glossary of human motivation. It has provided compelling challenges to artists in every generation. Medieval miniatures, modern painting, and sculpture have drawn their subject matter from it. The *Shahname* was both the first literary text to be illustrated, and the one whose illustration produced some of the greatest monuments of Islamic bookmaking and illustration. The influence of the *Shahname* on Iranian cultural life has been simply incalculable. It is one of the two or three most important works in a long and unusually rich literary tradition.

Nor has the *Shahname*'s influence been restricted to that of the Iranian nation alone, anymore than has Homer's to Greece. Ferdowsi's recension of the *Shahname* appeared just as Persian poetry was undergoing the remarkable efflorescence that allowed it first to rival and then to supersede Arabic poetry in the eastern Islamic world. Persian poetry was widely read and imitated in courts from Istanbul to Delhi, and exerted a formative influence on poetry in both Ottoman Turkish and Urdu.

The Language of the Shahname

The language of the *Shahname* is called New or Modern Persian to distinguish it from two earlier stages of the language: (1) Old Persian, a contemporary and cousin of Sanskrit and Avestan, and (2) Middle Persian, the language, or group of languages, that was current in Iran from roughly the time of Alexander to the Islamic invasion. The term New Persian is misleading in that it is used to designate the language throughout the entire thousand-year period of classical Persian literature. The language of contemporary Iran is known as Modern Persian. It would be more accurate to say that the language of the *Shahname*, and of classical poetry generally, is a special poetic dialect of Persian that has the same relationship to the language of today's Iran that Shakespeare's language does to the English we speak. The language of the *Shahname* represents an early and special form of this dialect. It retains a number of words and grammatical forms from Middle Persian that would have seemed archaic even to Ferdowsi's contemporaries, and is also virtually free of words borrowed from Arabic, even though Arabic loans words were common in the poetic dialect in use in the court.

The poetic form of the *Shahname* is a rhyming couplet of roughly ten syllables. The nearest equivalent to the Persian couplet in English is the heroic couplet. In both, the poetic unit is a pair of lines, marked by rhyme, and usually by syntactic divisions as well. The principal difference between the two is that in Persian, enjambment is virtually unheard of. While a sentence may run on for three lines, or even more on rare occasions, each clause of that sentence ends with the line. For example:

> Rostám, when he looked on her angel face,
> And saw in her a share of every art,
> And that she'd given him some news of Rakhsh,
> He saw no end to this that was not good.

The other striking difference between the two is that Persian poetic meters are based exclusively on syllable length. Syllables are measured as short ($\smile$), long ($-$), or overlong ($\overset{\frown}{\smile}$), and various combinations of these units make up the feet from which the many Persian meters are composed. Each meter has a name, and that of the meter of the *Shahname*, and, indeed, of most heroic poems in Persian, is *motaqareb*. This meter is composed of three feet of $|\smile--|$ (short + long + long) and one of $|\smile-|$ (short + long): $|\smile--|\smile--|\smile--|\smile-|$. Because the unit of measure is length not number, and a single overlong syllable may be counted as two syllables, the length of a line of *motaqareb* may vary from eight to eleven syllables although ten is the most common. Of the twenty-eight lines that make up the prologue of the poem, seventeen have ten syllables, five have eleven, three have nine, and three have eight. Stress is not included as a part of the metrical system. There are four or five stresses per line, but the placement of these stresses varies from foot to foot.

Rhyme in Persian is essentially what it is in English. Persian, however, has a preference for multiple rhymes, for a rhyme that consists of a sequence of two or more syllables. Moreover, Persian has a strong predilection for syntactic and phonetic parallels

between the two lines that make up a couplet. Here are the first
three couplets of the poem by way of example:

> ágar tónd bádi bár ayad ze k*ónj*
> be khák áfkanad nárasidé tor*ónj*
>
> setámkaré khanímesh ár dad*gár*
> honarmánd danímesh ár bí hon*ár*
>
> ágar márg dádast bíd*ad chíst*
> ze dád in hame báng o fary*ád chíst*
>
> What if a fierce and vagrant wind springs up,
> And casts a green unripened fruit to earth.
> Shall we call this a tyrant's act, or just?
> Shall we consider it as right or wrong?
> If death is just, how can this not be so?
> Why then lament and wail at what is just?

In the second couplet each word in the second line has the same
number of syllables as the word parallel to it in the first, and
there is a sequence of four syllables in the middle of the line that
differs only in the consonant that begins them (*khanimesh ar,
danimesh ar*). And the rhyme of the third couplet is a phrase
of two syllables.

The Present Translation

Ferdowsi's rendering of the tragic encounter of son and father
attracted the attention of poets in Europe from their discovery
of it. The first English translation was made by James Atkinson
and was published with the Persian text in Calcutta in 1814.
This was also the first English translation of a complete story
from the *Shahname*. Other translations into English and the
major European languages followed. Matthew Arnold composed
a neo-Homeric imitation of the story, which he gave the same
title as the original work, "Sohrab and Rustum." As interest in
the *Shahname* grew, so did the ambition of translators, and by
the beginning of the twentieth century this massive work had
been rendered in its entirety into French, German, Italian, and
English.

For the most part, the nineteenth-century English translators chose a language that was true both to the form of the original and to the archaic quality of its language. Theirs, however, was an age that allowed translators the freedom to alter texts to suit their own talents and sensibilities. Thus, Atkinson adds lines, indicated below by italics, to express Rakhsh's sense of freedom when Rostám releases him to graze after his hunt:

> The Warrior's steed, for strength and form renown'd
> Stray'd o'er the plain with flowery herbage crown'd
> *Encumbering arms no more his sides opprest,*
> *No folding mail confin'd his ample chest,*
> *Gallant and free, he left the Champion's side,*
> *And cropp'd the mead, or sought the rippling tide.*

Another translator, William Tulloh Robertson, whose version of Sohráb appeared in 1829, was sufficiently incensed by Rostám's treatment of his son to castigate him in the prologue:

> Ye who have listened to my other lays
> Of fields of battle fought in former days,
> Attentive listen to the tale I tell
> Of Roostum and Soohrab in combat fell—
> A tale pathetic and affecting hear,
> As well adapted to extract a tear,
> *As suited to arouse indignant ire,*
> *In tender hearts, against a cruel sire,*
> *Dishonoured Roostum—whom I cruel brand,*
> *Though justice he hath dealt with equal hand*
> *And call dishonoured, shorn of honor's name,*
> *Though he hath borne an honourable fame.*

By the early 1900s when the Warners undertook what has remained the only translation of the whole of the *Shahname* into English, a more scholarly attitude prevailed, and their work is free of such idiosyncracies. They also render the *Shahname* into blank verse rather than couplets. However, like earlier translators, they preserved the archaic flavor of the original:

> I tell what *rustic bard* and *archimage*
> Told from the legends of a *bygone* age:—
> One *morn* in *dudgeon* Rustam rose to hunt,

Girt him, filled up his quiver, mounted Rakhsh,
And *hied* him to the marches of Turán,
A savage Lion prowling after prey.

The style is one that was current in their day, but it has since
fallen from favor. Such conscious archaizing now sounds artificial
and even comic.

I have sought to provide a version of the tale that sounds
like modern English, but which gives some sense of the formal
tone of the original. I have used blank verse rather than a freer
line because I think readers need a regular rhythmic pattern
to sustain them through a long narrative. I have also been
truer to syntactic divisions than the Warners were, and have
tried to translate line for line, if not word for word. Epic has
its flat moments. The poet must get his hero on and off his
horse as well as in and out of battle, and actions both heroic
and ordinary require the same number of words to express.
The temptation for the translator is to shorten these passages
of *recitatio* and expand the arias, but to do so gives a false
sense of the movement of the poem. My translation differs from
earlier versions in another way. It is based on an older and more
carefully edited manuscript, which was unavailable to earlier
translators. To be more specific, the Persian text given here
is that of the British Museum manuscript dated 1276–77 (A.H.
675) and presented in the Moscow edition. On the few occasions
when I have taken readings or lines from other manuscripts I
have indicated where and why I have done so in the notes. While
some of the additions made by later copyists may belong to the
original in some sense, for the most part they are expansions
and repetitions that were added, I feel, not to improve the text
but simply to give the copyist or reciter a more personal claim
upon it. My own preference is for the leaner text of the earliest
manuscripts. The sections of the poem have no titles in the
British Museum manuscript. Other manuscripts add titles, and
I have done so for my translation as well. These titles vary from
manuscript to manuscript.

The Persian text of the story is printed on facing pages
because to do so makes this translation more useful to the many

who know one language well but not the other. However, the English text is not meant to be the literal equivalent of the Persian. I have tried to be true to the original, but mine is a poetic translation, not a photographic one. All translators hope their work will lead readers back to the original, I know I do. There must be few who think a prosaic translation is more likely to do so than a poetic one.

A Note on Transliteration

Persian names are generally stressed on the last syllable. I have translated with that rhythm in mind and indicated where primary word stress should fall by an accent mark (´). The name of the paramount hero of the *Shahname* is Rostám not Róstam ("roast'em").

The "kh" in Rakhsh is a velar fricative pronounced like the (ch) in *Bach* or *Rachmaninoff*, the (j) in *frijoles*, or the (kh) in *la khaim*. The pronunciation of the other consonants is essentially that of English. The vowels of Persian should be pronounced as follows:

u	dude
e	end
i	see
o	ode
a	either cat or calm*

*There seems to me no satisfactory way to distinguish between these two sounds in normal English orthography, and I am reluctant to import a special letter—such as æ—for the purpose. However, in the glossary that follows the translation, I have indicated where (a) should be pronounced like the a in "cat" and where like that in "calm."

Note to the Revised Edition

When I first worked on this translation, I did not anticipate that it would be published together with the original text. While the British Museum manuscript was the base from which I worked, I also translated a number of passages from the Minovi edition, and thus there were some discrepancies between the original and the translation. The translation has been corrected here to conform to the British Museum manuscript.

Also, although I set out to render the text into idiomatic modern English, I couldn't resist the siren call of an occasional archaism. These I have winnowed out. For the rest, in making revisions I have had before me the translator's familiar twin goals of fluency and fidelity.

Ferdowsi's millenary has passed since this translation was first published, and it brought with it a substantial increase in the always voluminous publications on Ferdowsi. Among these new works are the first two monographs on Ferdowsi in English: *Epic and Sedition: The Case of Ferdowsi's Shahnamah* by Dick Davis (Fayetteville: University of Arkansas Press, 1992) and *Poet and Hero in the Persian Book of Kings* by Olga M. Davidson (Ithaca, N.Y.: Cornell University Press, 1994).

The Tragedy of Sohráb and Rostám

اگر تند بادی برآید ز کنج

بخاک افگند نارسیده ترنج

ستم کاره خوانیمش ار دادگر

هنرمند دانیمش ار بی هنر

اگر مرگ دادست بیداد چیست

ز داد این همه بانگ و فریاد چیست

ازاین راز جان تو آگاه نیست

بدین پرده اندر ترا راه نیست

۵   همه تا در آز رفته فراز

بکس بر نشد این در راز باز

برفتن مگر بهتر آیدش جای

چو آرام یابد بدیگر سرای

دم مرگ چون آتش هولناک

ندارد ز برناو فرتوت باک

درین جای رفتن نه جای درنگ

2

§*Prologue*

What if a wind springs up quite suddenly,

And casts a green unripened fruit to earth.

Shall we call this a tyrant's act, or just?

Shall we consider it as right, or wrong?

If death is just, how can this not be so?

Why then lament and wail at what is just?

Your soul knows nothing of this mystery;

You cannot see what lies beyond this veil.

5 Though all descend to face that greedy door,

For none has it revealed its secrets twice.

Perhaps he'll like the place he goes to better,

And in that other house he may find peace.

Death's breath is like a fiercely raging fire

That has no fear of either young or old.

Here in this place of passing, not delay,

بر اسب فنا گر کشد مرگ تنگ

چنان دان که دادست و بیداد نیست

چو داد آمدش جای فریاد نیست

۱۰   جوانی و پیری بنزدیک مرگ

یکی دان چو اندر بدن نیست برگ

دل از نور ایمان گر آگندهٔ

ترا خامشی به که تو بندهٔ

برین کار یزدان ترا راز نیست

اگر جانت با دیو انباز نیست

بگیتی دران کوش چون بگذری

سرانجام نیکی بَر خود بری

کنون رزم سهراب رانم نخست

ازان کین که او با پدر چون بجست

۱۵   ز گفتار دهقان یکی داستان

بپیوندم از گفتهٔ باستان

ز موبد برین گونه برداشت یاد

که رستم یکی روز از بامداد

غمی بد دلش ساز نخچیر کرد

کمر بست و ترکش پر از تیر کرد

سوی مرز توران چو بنهاد روی

چو شیر دژ آگاه نخچیر جوی

چو نزدیکی مرز توران رسید

Should death cinch tight the saddle on its steed,

Know this, that it is just, and not unjust.

There's no disputing justice when it comes.

10 Destruction knows both youth and age as one,

For nothing that exists will long endure.

If you can fill your heart with faith's pure light,

Silence befits you best, since you're His slave.

You do not understand God's mysteries,

Unless your soul is partners with some *div*.

Strive here within the world as you pass through,

And in the end bear virtue in your heart.

Now I'll relate the story of Sohráb,

And how he came to battle with his father.

§ *The Beginning*

15 In the *dehqáns'* stories there is a tale that I

Have versified from ancient narratives.

The *mobad* starts his recollections thus—[1]

Rostám one day just as the sun rose up,

Was sad at heart, and so prepared to hunt.

He armed himself, put arrows in his quiver,

And like a fearsome lion on the chase,

He galloped toward the borders of Turán.

As he approached the Turkish borderlands,

بیابان سراسر پر از گور دید

۲۰ بر افروخت چون گل رخ تاج بخش

بخندید و ز جای برکند رخش

بتیر و کمان و بگرز و کمند

بیفگند بر دشت نخچیر چند

زخاشاک وز خار وشاخ درخت

یکی آتشی بر فروزید سخت

چو آتش پراگنده شد پیلتن

درختی بجست از در باب زن

یکی نره گوری بزد بردرخت

که در چنگ او پرّ مرغی نسخت

۲۵ چو بریان شد از هم بکند و بخورد

ز مغز استخوانش برآورد گرد

بخفت وبرآسود از روزگار

چمان و چران رخش در مرغزار

سواران ترکان تنی هفت و هشت

بران دشت نخچیر گه بر گذشت

یکی اسپ دیدند در مرغزار

بگشتند گرد لب جویبار

چو بر دشت مر رخش را یافتند

سوی بند کردنش بشتافتند

۳۰ گرفتند و بردند پویان بشهر

همی هریک از رخش جستند بهر

He saw the plain was filled with onagers.[2]

20   The Giver of the Crown glowed like a rose.[3]

He laughed aloud and spurred Rakhsh from his place.[4]

With bow and arrow, and with mace and rope,

He brought down many onagers upon

The plain. Then from dead branches, brush, and thorns,

Rostám built up a fiercely blazing fire.

When the fire had spread, the huge hero wrenched a tree

Out of the ground to serve him as a spit.

He placed a heavy stallion on that tree,

That was a feather in his palm, no more.

25   When it was done he tore its limbs apart,

And wolfed it down, the marrow bones and all.

Rostám then slept and rested from the hunt.

Nearby Rakhsh wandered, grazing in a meadow.

Turkish horsemen, some seven or eight, passed by

That plain and hunting ground; and as they rode

They spied a horse's tracks, and turned aside

To follow them along the river's bank.

When they found Rakhsh grazing on the plain,

They raced ahead to snare him with their ropes.

30   Once he was caught, they bore him galloping

Toward the town; each eager for his share.

چو بیدار شد رستم از خواب خوش

بکار آمدش بارهٔ دست کش

غمی گشت چون بارگی را نیافت

سراسیمه سوی سمنگان شتافت

همی گفت کاکنون پیاده دوان

کجا پویم از ننگ تیره روان

چه گویند گردان که اسپش که برد

تهمتن بدین سان بخفت و بمرد

۳۵   کنون رفت باید به بیچارگی

سپردن بغم دل بیکبارگی

کنون بست باید سلیح و کمر

بجایی نشانش بیابم مگر

همی رفت زین سان پراندوه ورنج

تن اندر عنا و دل اندر شکنج

چو نزدیک شهر سمنگان رسید

خبر زو بشاه و بزرگان رسید

که آمد پیاده گو تاج بخش

بنخچیر گه زو رمیدست رخش

۴۰   پذیره شدندش بزرگان و شاه

کسی کو بسر بر نهادی کلاه

بدو گفت شاه سمنگان چه بود

که یارست باتو نبرد آزمود

درین شهر ما نیکخواه توایم

Rostám when he awoke from his sweet sleep,

Had need of his well-trained and ready steed.

He was distressed to find that Rakhsh was gone,

And quickly turned his face toward Semengán.

Rebuking himself, he said, "Now I'm unhorsed,

Where shall I flee from this soul-blackening shame?

What will the heroes say? 'They stole his horse.

Thus did he sleep. Thus did he lose his life.'

35 Now I must travel on in wretched state,

Abandoning my heart and soul to grief.

Now I must buckle on both arms and belt.

Perhaps I'll find his tracks along the way."

And so he journeyed on with aching heart,

His body bent with weariness and shame.

§*In Semengán*

As he drew near to Semengán, the shah

And nobles heard, "The Giver of the Crown

Approaches now on foot. While they were on

A hunt, the shining Rakhsh fled from his hand."

40 The shah and all his nobles greeted him,

All those who wore a crown upon their heads.

The shah of Semengán inquired of him,

"What can this mean? Who's dared to challenge you?

Within this city we are all your friends.

ستاده بفرمان و راه توایم

تن و خواسته زیر فرمان تست

سر ارجمندان و جان آن تست

چو رستم بگفتار او بنگرید

ز بدها گمانیش کوتاه دید

۴۵   بدو گفت رخشم بدین مرغزار

ز من دور شد بی لگام و فسار

کنون تا سمنگان نشان پی است

وز آنجا کجا جویبارونی است

ترا باشد ار بازجویی سپاس

بباشم بپاداش نیکی شناس

گر ایدونک ماند ز من ناپدید

سران را بسی سر بباید برید

بدو گفت شاه ای سزاوار مرد

نیارد کسی باتو این کار کرد

۵۰   تو مهمان من باش وتندی مکن

بکام تو گردد سراسر سخن

یک امشب بمی شاد داریم دل

وز اندیشه آزاد داریم دل

نماند پی رخش فرّخ نهان

چنان بارهٔ نامدار جهان

تهمتن بگفتار او شاد شد

روانش ز اندیشه آزاد شد

سزا دید رفتن سوی خان او

We stand beside your path, alert to serve.

You may command our persons as our wealth.

These nobles' heads and hearts belong to you."

Rostám considered well his words and saw

That he'd small cause for his distrust and doubt.

45 He answered him and said, "While in the field,

Rakhsh fled from me, with neither bit nor reins.

His tracks come to the city's edge; and on

The other side, there's only reeds and swamp.

Find him and you will have my thanks. In my

Reward I'll show you all my gratitude.

But if you don't, and he remains unfound,

Then many noble lords will lose their heads."

To him the shah replied, "Oh worthy man!

No one would dare to do such things to you.

50 Don't act in haste, but be my welcome guest.

This matter will conclude as you desire.

Tonight let us rejoice our hearts with wine,

And keep them free of evil thoughts as well.

The tracks of shining Rakhsh, a steed who is

Well known to all, will not stay hidden long."

Brave Tahamtán rejoiced to hear his words.[5]

His soul was freed of all disquietude.

It now seemed right to him to visit in

شد از مژده دلشاد مهمان او

۵۵   سپهبد بدو داد در کاخ جای

همی بود در پیش او بر بپای

ز شهر و ز لشکر مهانرا بخواند

سزاوار با او بشادی نشاند

گسارندۀ باده آورد ساز

سیه چشم و گل رخ بتان طراز

نشستند با رودسازان بهم

بدان تا تهمتن نباشد دژم

چو شد مست و هنگام خواب آمدش

همی از نشستن شتاب آمدش

۶۰   سزاوار او جای آرام و خواب

بیاراست و بنهاد مشک و گلاب

چو یک بهره ازتیره شب در گذشت

شباهنگ بر چرخ گردان بگشت

سخن گفتن آمد نهفته براز

در خواب گه نرم کردند باز

یکی بنده شمعی معنبر بدست

خرامان بیامد ببالین مست

پس پرده اندر یکی ماه روی

چو خورشید تابان پر از رنگ وبوی

۶۵   دو ابرو کمان و دوگیسو کمند

His home. This happy news made him his guest.

55 The ruler then gave him a place within

His castle keep, and waited by his side.

He summoned all the city's great, those who

Were worthy to be seated at the feast.

The bearer of the wine, the harper too,

And dark-eyed, rose-cheeked idols of Taráz,

All joined with the musicians gathered there,

To see that great Rostám should not be sad.

When he grew drunk, and sleep came to his eyes,

He wished to leave the feast and seek his rest.

60 They led him to a place fit for a prince,

A quiet chamber sweet with scent and musk.

§ *Tahminé*

And when one watch had passed on that dark night,

And Sirius rose on the heavens' wheel.

The sound of secret voices could be heard.

The chamber door was opened quietly.

A single slave, a scented candle in

Her hand, came to the pillow of Rostám.

Behind the slave, a moon-faced maid appeared,[6]

Adorned and scented like the shining sun.

65 Her eyebrows bows, her tresses lassoes coiled,

ببالا بکردار سرو بلند

روانش خرد بود و تن جان پاک

تو گفتی که بهره ندارد ز خاک

از او رستم شیردل خیره ماند

برو بر جهان آفرین را بخواند

بپرسید زو گفت نام تو چیست

چه جویی شب تیره کام تو چیست

چنین داد پاسخ که تهمینه ام

تو گویی که از غم بدو نیمه ام

۷۰ یکی دخت شاه سمنگان منم

ز پشت هژبر و پلنگان منم

بگیتی ز خوبان مرا جفت نیست

چو من زیر چرخ کبود اندکیست

کس از پرده بیرون ندیدی مرا

نه هرگز کس آوا شنیدی مرا

بکردار افسانه از هرکسی

شنیدم همی داستانت بسی

که از شیر و دیو ونهنگ وپلنگ

نترسی و هستی چنین تیز چنگ

۷۵ شب تیره تنها بتوران شوی

بگردی بران مرز و هم بغنوی

بتنها یکی گور بریان کنی

هوا را بشمشیر گریان کنی

هر آنگه که گرز تو بیند بجنگ

In stature like a slender cypress tree.

Her soul was wisdom and her body seemed

Of spirit pure, as though not made of earth.

Amazed, Rostám the fearless lion-heart,

Cried out the Maker's name on seeing her.

He questioned her, and asked, "What is your name?

Here in the dead of night, what do you seek?"

She answered him, "My name is Tahminé

It seems my heart's been rent in two by grief.

70 The daughter of the shah of Semengán,

From lions and from tigers comes my seed.

In all the world no beauty is my match.

Few are my like beneath the azure wheel.

Outside these walls, there's none who's looked on me.

Nor has my voice been heard by any ear.

From everyone I've heard such tales of you—

So wonderful they seemed to me like myths.

They say you fear no leopard and no *div*.

No crocodile or lion is so fierce.

75 At night alone, you journey to Turán,

And wander freely there, and even sleep.

You spit an onager with just one hand,

And with your sword you cause the air to weep.

When you approach them with your mace in hand,

بدرّد دل شیر و چنگ پلنگ

برهنه چو تیغ تو بیند عقاب

نیارد بنخچیر کردن شتاب

نشان کمند تو دارد هژبر

ز بیم سنان تو خون بارد ابر

۸۰   چو این داستانها شنیدم ز تو

بسی لب بدندان گزیدم ز تو

بجستم همی کفت و یال و برت

بدین شهر کرد ایزد آبشخورت

ترا ام کنون گر بخواهی مرا

نبیند جزین مرغ و ماهی مرا

یکی آنک برتو چنین گشته ام

خرد را ز بهر هوا کشته ام

ودیگر که از تو مگر کردگار

نشاند یکی پورم اندر کنار

۸۵   مگر چون تو باشد بمردی وزور

سپهرش دهد بهره کیوان و هور

سه دیگر که اسپت بجای آورم

سمنگان همه زیر پای آورم

چو رستم برانسان پری چهره دید

زهر دانشی نزد او بهره دید

ودیگر که از رخش داد آگهی

ندید ایچ فرجام جز فرّهی

بخوشنودی و رای و فرمان اوی

The leopard rends his claws, the lion his heart.

The eagle when he sees your naked blade,

Fears to take wing and fly off to the hunt.

The tiger's skin is branded by your rope.

The clouds weep blood in fear of your sharp lance.

80   As I would listen to these tales of you,

I'd bite my lip in wonder, and yearn

To look upon those shoulders and that chest.

And then Izád sent you to Semengán.[7]

I'm yours now should you want me, and, if not,

None but the fish and birds will see my face.

First, because I do so long for you

That I've slain reason for my passion's sake.

And next, perhaps the Maker of the World

Will place a son from you within my womb.

85   Perhaps he'll be like you in manliness

And strength, a child of Saturn and the Sun.

And third, that I may bring your horse to you,

I'll search throughout the whole of Semengán."

Rostám looked on her angel face, seeing

In her a share of every grace and art.

Moreover, she'd given him some news of Rakhsh.

He saw no end to this that was not good.

So as she wished, and with good will and joy,

بخوبی بیاراست پیمان اوی

۹۰ چو انباز او گشت بااو براز

ببود آن شب تیره دیر ودراز

چو خورشید تابان ز چرخ بلند

همی خواست افگند رخشان کمند

ببازوی رستم یکی مهره بود

که آن مهره اندر جهان شهره بود

بدو داد وگفتش که این را بدار

اگر دختر آرد ترا روزگار

بگیر وبگیسوی او بر بدوز

بنیک اختر وفال گیتی فروز

۹۵ ور ایدونک آید ز اختر پسر

ببندش ببازو نشان پدر

ببالای سام نریمان بود

بمردی و خوی کریمان بود

فرود آرد ازابر پرّان عقاب

نتابد بتندی براو آفتاب

همی بود آن شب بر ماه روی

همی گفت از هرسخن پیش اوی

چو خورشید رخشنده شد بر سپهر

بیاراست روی زمین را بمهر

۱۰۰ بررستم آمد گرانمایه شاه

بپرسیدش از خواب و آرام گاه

Rostám sealed firm his bond with her that night.[8]

90 And when in secret she'd become his mate,

The night that followed lasted late and long.

But then at last, from high above the world,

The radiant sun cast down his shining rope.

Upon his arm Rostám had placed a seal,

A jewel that was famous through the world.

He gave it to her as he said, "Keep this.

And if the times should bring a girl to you,

Then take this gem and plait it in her hair—

A world-illumining omen of good luck.

95 But if the star of fate should send a son,

Then bind this father's token to his arm.

He'll be as tall as Sam or Narimán,[9]

In strength and manliness a noble youth,

He'll bring the eagle from the clouds above.

The sun will not look harshly on this boy."

Rostám conversed that night with his new moon,

And spoke with her of all he'd known and seen.

The radiant sun at last rose to the heights

And shed his glorious light upon the earth.

100 The worthy shah approached the chamber of

Rostám, to ask if he had rested well.

چو این گفته شد مژده دادش برخش

برو شادمان شد دل تاج بخش

بیامد بمالید و زین برنهاد

شد از رخش رخشان و از شاه شاد

چو نه ماه بگذشت بردخت شاه

یکی پورش آمد چو تابنده ماه

تو گفتی گو پیلتن رستمست

وگر سام شیرست و گر نیرمست

۱۰۵   چو خندان شد وچهره شاداب کرد

ورا نام تهمینه سهراب کرد

چو یک ماه شد همچو یک سال بود

برش چون بر رستم زال بود

چو سه ساله شد زخم چوگان گرفت

بپنجم دل تیر وپیکان گرفت

چو ده ساله شد زان زمین کس نبود

که یارست بااو نبرد آزمود

بر مادر آمد بپرسید زوی

بدو گفت گستاخ با من بگوی

۱۱۰   که من چون ز همشیرگان برترم

همی بآسمان اندرآید سرم

ز تخم کیم وزکدامین گهر

چه گویم چو پرسد کسی از پدر

گر این پرسش ازمن بماند نهان

And this once said, he gave him news of Rakhsh.

The Giver of the Crown rejoiced at this.

He went and stroked his steed and saddled him,

Then thanked the shah, well pleased at his return.

§ *The Birth of Sohráb*

When nine months passed for Tahminé, she bore

A healthy boy whose face shone like the moon.

It seemed he was the *pahlaván* Rostám,

Or that he was the lion Sam, or Narimán.

105 Because he laughed and had a cheerful face,

His mother called him by the name Sohráb.[10]

In but a single month he'd grown a year.

His chest was like Rostám's, the son of Zal.

At three he learned the game of polo, and

At five he mastered bow and javelin.

When he was ten, in all of Semengán

Not one would dare to meet him in the field.

Sohráb went to his mother, Tahminé,

To question her, "Tell me the truth," he said.

110 I'm taller than the boys who nursed with me.

It seems my head can touch the very sky.

Whose seed am I, and of what family?

When asked, 'Who is your father?' What shall I say?

If you should keep this answer from me now,

نمانم ترا زنده اندر جهان

بدو گفت مادر که بشنو سخن

بدین شادمان باش و تندی مکن

تو پور گوپیلتن رستمی

ز دستان سامی و از نیرمی

۱۱۵   ازیرا سرت ز آسمان برترست

که تخم تو زان نامور گوهرست

جهان آفرین تا جهان آفرید

سواری چو رستم نیامد پدید

چو سام نریمان بگیتی نبود

سرش را نیارست گردون بسود

یکی نامه از رستم جنگ جوی

بیاورد وبنمود پنهان بدوی

سه یاقوت رخشان بسه مهره زر

از ایران فرستاده بودش پدر

۱۲۰   بدو گفت افراسیاب این سخن

نباید که داند ز سر تابین

پدر گر شناسد که تو زین نشان

شدستی سر افراز گردنکشان

چو داند بخواندت نزدیک خویش

دل مادرت گردد از درد ریش

چنین گفت سهراب کاندر جهان

کسی این سخن را ندارد نهان

بزرگان جنگ آور از باستان

I will not leave you in this world alive."

His mother answered him, "Don't speak so harshly,

But hear my words and be rejoiced by them.

Your father is the *pahlaván* Rostám.

Your ancestors are Sam and Narimán.

115   And so it is your head can touch the sky.

You are descended from that famous line.

Since first the World Creator made the earth.

There's been no other horseman like Rostám.

Nor one like Sam the son of Narimán.

The turning sphere does not dare brush his head."

And then she brought a letter from his father,

Rostám, and showed it secretly to him.

Enclosed with it Rostám had also sent

Three shining emeralds in three golden seals.

120   "Afrasiyáb must never know of this,"

She said, "he must not hear a single word.

Your father, if he learns that you've become

A brave and noble warrior like this,

Will call you to his side, I know,

And then your mother's heart will break."

The bold Sobráb replied, "In all the world

No man could keep a secret such as this.

From ancient times till now, those great in war

ز رستم زنند این زمان داستان

۱۲۵   نبرده نژادی که چونین بود

نهان کردن از من ز چه آیین بود

کنون من ز ترکان جنگ آوران

فراز آورم لشکری بی کران

برانگیزم از گاه کاوس را

از ایران ببرّم پی طوس را

برستم دهم تخت و گرز وکلاه

نشانمش بر گاه کاوس شاه

از ایران بتوران شوم جنگ جوی

ابا شاه روی اندر آرم بروی

۱۳۰   بگیرم سرتخت افراسیاب

سرنیزه بگذارم از آفتاب

چو رستم پدر باشد و من پسر

نباید بگیتی کسی تاجور

چو روشن بود روی خورشید وماه

ستاره چرا بر فرازد کلاه

ز هرسو سپه شد برو انجمن

که هم با گهر بود و هم تیغ زن

خبر شد بنزدیک افراسیاب

که افگند سهراب کشتی برآب

۱۳۵   هنوز از دهن بوی شیر آیدش

Recite for all the tales of brave Rostám.

125 When I have such a warlike lineage,

For me to keep it hidden can't be right.

Now from among the warlike Turks I will

Amass an army boundless as the sea.

I'll drive Kavús from off his throne,

And from Irán I'll scour all trace of Tus.

To brave Rostám I'll give throne, mace, and crown,

And seat him in the place of Shah Kavús.

Then from Irán I will attack Turán,

There to confront the shah, Afrasiyáb.

130 I'll rout his army and I'll seize his throne.

I'll thrust my lance's tip above the sun.

When Rostám is the father, I the son,

Who else in all the world should wear a crown?

When sun and moon illuminate the sky,

Why should the stars parade their crowns at night?"

From every side an army flocked to him,

Who all were noble men, brave swordsmen too.

§*The Campaign Begins*

This news was brought to Shah Afrásiyáb,

"Sohráb has launched his boat upon the stream.

135 The smell of milk still lingers on his mouth,

همی رای شمشیر و تیر آیدش

زمین را بخنجر بشوید همی

کنون رزم کاوس جوید همی

سپاه انجمن شد برو بربسی

نیاید همی یادش از هرکسی

سخن زین درازی چه باید کشید

همی برتر از گوهر آید پدید

چو افراسیاب آن سخنها شنود

خوش آمدش خندید و شادی نمود

۱۴۰   ز لشکر گزید از دلاور سران

کسی کو گراید بگرز گران

ده و دو هزار از دلیران گرد

چو هومان و مر بارمان را سپرد

بگردان لشکر سپهدار گفت

که این راز باید که ماند نهفت

چو روی اندر آرند هر دو بروی

تهمتن بود بی گمان چاره جوی

پدر را نباید که داند پسر

که بندد دل و جان بمهر پدر

۱۴۵   مگر کان دلاور گو سال خورد

شود کشته بر دست این شیرمرد

ازان پس بسازید سهراب را

ببندید یک شب برو خواب را

برفتند بیدار دو پهلوان

And yet he thinks of weapons and of war.

Since he would scour the whole earth with his sword,

He seeks to fight a war with Shah Kavús.

A legion of soldiers have gathered to his side,

And he gives thought to no one else at all.

But why should speech be thus drawn out so long.

His prowess far exceeds that of his birth." [11]

When Shah Afrasiyáb had heard these words,

He was well pleased and laughed and showed his joy.

140 Then from among the army's valiant chief,

Those with the strength to wield a heavy mace,

He chose twelve thousand braves, men like Humán,

These men he then entrusted to Barmán.

Afrasiyáb addressed his generals, saying,

"This secret must not ever come to light.

When these two face each other on the field,

The bold Rostám will surely try some ruse.

The boy must not recognize his father,

Or else his love will bind his heart to him.

145 Rather, that brave and ancient *pahlaván*

Must lose his life to this young lion-heart.

Then later on destroy the fierce Sohráb.

Bind him one night forever in his dreams."

Alertly both the warriors went off

بنزدیک سهراب روشن روان

بپیش اندرون هدیهٔ شهریار

ده اسپ وده استر بزین وببار

ز پیروزه تخت و ز بیجاده تاج

سر تاج زر پایهٔ تخت عاج

۱۵۰ یکی نامه با لابه و دلپسند

نبشته بنزدیک آن ارجمند

که گر تخت ایران بچنگ آوری

زمانه بر آساید از داوری

ازین مرز تا آن بسی راه نیست

سمنگان و ایران و توران یکیست

فرستمت هر چند باید سپاه

تو برتخت بنشین وبر نه کلاه

بتوران چو هومان و چون بارمان

دلیر و سپهبد نبد بی گمان

۱۵۵ فرستادم اینک بفرمان تو

که باشند یک چند مهمان تو

اگر جنگ جویی تو جنگ آورند

جهان بر بداندیش تنگ آورند

چنین نامه و خلعت شهریار

ببردند باساز چندان سوار

بسهراب آگاهی آمد ز راه

ز هومان و از بارمان و سپاه

پذیره بشد با نیا همچو باد

To meet Sohráb of the enlightened mind.

They took with them the gift their monarch sent:

Twelve thousand horses, camels, and their gear;

A throne of turquoise with four silver legs;

A ruby crown whose crest was all of gold.

150　They brought as well a letter filled with praise,

That he had written to that worthy youth.

If you can seize the throne of all Irán,

You'll ease the disputations of our times.

The road that lies between us is not long.

Irán, Turán, and Semengán are one.

I'll send whatever troops you may require.

You sit upon the throne and wear the crown.

For bravery and generalship, Turán

Has none to match Humán and brave Barmán.

155　*I've sent them now to be at your command.*

Let them abide there for a time as guests.

If you seek war, they'll fight for you, and make

The world too narrow for your enemies.

A letter such as this, and royal robes,

They took with them, and gear for many knights.

　　Word of Humán, Barmán, and all their troops

Soon reached Sohráb from lookouts on the road.

He and his grandfather went to greet this host.

سپه دید چندان دلش گشت شاد

۱۶۰   چو هومان ورا دید بایال وکفت

فرو ماند هومان ازو در شگفت

بدو داد پس نامهٔ شهریار

ابا هدیه واسپ واستر ببار

جهانجوی چون نامهٔ شاه خواند

ازان جایگه تیز لشکر براند

کسی را نبد پای باو بجنگ

اگر شیر پیش آمدی گر پلنگ

دژی بود کش خواندندی سپید

بران دژ بد ایرانیان را امید

۱۶۵   نگهبان دژ رزم دیده هجیر

که بازور و دل بود وبا داروگیر

هنوز آنزمان گستهم خرد بود

بخردی گراینده و گرد بود

یکی خواهرش بود گرد وسوار

بداندیش و گردنکش و نامدار

چو سهراب نزدیکی دژ رسید

هجیر دلاور سپه را بدید

نشست ازبر بادپای چو گرد

ز دژ رفت پویان بدشت نبرد

۱۷۰   چو سهراب جنگ آور اورا بدید

برآشفت و شمشیر کین برکشید

ز لشکر برون تاخت برسان شیر

When he saw so many troops his heart rejoiced.

160 Humán, when he first saw his shoulders and

His massive chest, stood speechless in his awe.

He gave Sohráb the royal letter and

The horses, the camels, and their precious loads.

When that ambitious youth had read the words,

He quickly led his army from their camp.

For no one could stand up to him in battle,

No lion or leopard on the field of war.

There was a fortress which they called the White;

The hopes of all Irán were placed in it.

165 The battle-tried Hojír, a man of strength

And bravery, was keeper of the fort.

For in that time Gostáhm was still a youth,

Although a youth of bold, heroic bearing.

He had a warlike sister too, who was

Well known for her ferocity and strength.

The army of Sohráb approached the fort,

The brave Hojír observed the army there.

Swift as the wind he mounted on his horse,

And galloped out to battle from the fort.

170 When bold Sohráb saw that Hojír approached,

He flushed in rage and drew his vengeful sword,

And like a lion raced onto the field.

بپیش هجیر اندر آمد دلیر

چنین گفت با رزم دیده هجیر

که تنها بجنگ آمدی خیره خیر

چه مردی ونام ونژاد تو چیست

که زاینده را برتو باید گریست

هجیرش چنین داد پاسخ که بس

بترکی نباید مرا یار کس

۱۷۵   هجیر دلیر و سپهبد منم

سرت را هم اکنون ز تن بر کنم

فرستم بنزدیک شاه جهان

تنت را کنم زیر گل در نهان

بخندید سهراب کین گفت وگوی

بگوش آمدش تیز بنهاد روی

چنان نیزه بر نیزه برساختند

که از یکدگر باز نشناختند

یکی نیزه زد بر میانش هجیر

نیامد سنان اندرو جایگیر

۱۸۰   سنان باز پس کرد سهراب شیر

بن نیزه زد بر میان دلیر

ز زین بر گرفتش بکردار باد

نیامد همی زو بدلش ایچ یاد

ز اسپ اندر آمد نشست از برش

همی خواست از تن بریدن سرش

بپیچید و برگشت بردست راست

As he approached the battle-tried Hojír,

Sohráb the valiant called to him and said,

"Oh foolish man, to fight with me alone!

What is your name, and which your family?

Who is the mother that must weep for you?"

Hojír answered him in turn, "In all Turán

There can be few or none to equal me.

175   I am Hojír the brave, the army's chief.

I mean to tear your head off your body

And send it to the world's shah, Kay Kavús.

Your body will I hide beneath the earth."

When he had heard this boast, Sohráb just laughed

And galloped forward to attack Hojír.

So swiftly did they hurl their weapons that

The eye could not distinguish lance from lance.

One lance Hojír thrust at Sohráb, the point

Of which slid off his waist and did not stick.

180   Sohráb then seized the lance, reversed its butt,

And struck his chest a fierce and telling blow

That lifted him free of his horse's back

And stretched him stunned and gasping on the ground.

Sohráb sprang down and sat upon his chest,

Drawing his sword to sever head from trunk.

Hojír beneath him twisted to his right,

غمی شد ز سهراب و زنهار خواست

رها کرد ازو چنگ و زنهار داد

چو خوشنود شد پند بسیار داد

۱۸۵ ببستش ببند آنگهی رزمجوی

بنزدیک هومان فرستاد اوی

بدژ در چو آگه شدند از هجیر

که اورا گرفتند وبردند اسیر

خروش آمد و نالهٔ مرد و زن

که کم شد هجیر اندر آن انجمن

چو آگاه شد دختر گژدهم

که سالار آن انجمن گشت کم

زنی بود برسان گردی سوار

همیشه بجنگ اندرون نامدار

۱۹۰ کجا نام او بود گرد آفرید

زمانه ز مادر چنین ناورید

چنان ننگش آمد زکار هجیر

که شد لاله رنگش بکردار قیر

بپوشید درع سواران جنگ

نبود اندر آن کار جای درنگ

نهان کرد گیسو بزیر زره

بزد بر سر ترگ رومی گره

And in his fear he begged Sohráb for mercy.

The youth released his grip and spared his life.

Pleased with himself, he counseled him instead.

185 Then binding Hojír's hands with rope, he sent

Him as a captive to Humán.

Within the fort, when all had heard the news,

"Hojír's been taken captive by the Turks,"

They cried aloud, and men and women wept,

"The brave Hojír has now been lost to us."

§ *Gordafaríd*

The daughter of Gozhdáhm, when she was told

The leader of their company'd been lost;

And she was a woman who like a knight

Had gained renown in war, and who was called

190 Gordafaríd—for in her time there was[12]

No mother who had borne her like—she found

The conduct of Hojír so shameful that

The tulips in her cheeks turned black as pitch.

She wasted not a moment, but bound on

The coat of mail a horseman wears to fight.

She hid her hair beneath that coat of mail,

And tied a Roman helmet on her head.

فرود آمد از دژ بکردار شیر

کمر بر میان بادپایی بزیر

۱۹۵   بپیش سپاه اندر آمد چو گرد

چو رعد خروشان یکی ویله کرد

که گردان کدامند و جنگ آوران

دلیران وکارآزموده سران

چو سهراب شیراوژن اورا بدید

بخندید ولب را بدندان گزید

چنین گفت کامد دگر باره گور

بدام خداوند شمشیر و زور

پوشید خفتان و بر سرنهاد

یکی ترگ چینی بکردار باد

۲۰۰   بیامد دمان پیش گرد آفرید

چو دخت کمند افگن اورا بدید

کمان را بزه کرد وبگشاد بر

نبد مرغ را پیش تیرش گذر

بسهراب بر تیر باران گرفت

چپ وراست جنگ سواران گرفت

نگه کرد سهراب و آمدش ننگ

برآشفت و تیز اندر آمد بجنگ

سپر بر سرآورد و بنهاد روی

ز پیگار خون اندر آمد بجوی

۲۰۵   چو سهراب را دید گرد آفرید

که برسان آتش همی بر دمید

Then lionlike she raced down from the fort,

Girded for battle, and seated on the wind.

195 She faced the army like a warrior,

Roaring a challenge like a thunderbolt,

"Who are your heroes, who your *pahlaváns*,

And who your brave and battle-tested chiefs?"

Sohráb the lion-killer laughed when he

Saw her, and bit his lip in amazement.

"Another onager has rushed into

The trap set by the lord of mace and blade."

Swift as the wind he donned his armored shirt,

And bound a Chinese helmet on his head,

200 Then galloped out to meet Gordafaríd.

When that rope-hurling maid saw him approach,

She strung her heavy bow and drew a breath—

No bird escaped her arrows with its life.

She rained her darts upon Sohráb, and as

She rode, she dodged and feinted right and left.

Sohráb observed her charge and felt ashamed,

Then flushed with rage and galloped to the fray.

He lifted up his shield and charged his foe,

The blood of battle coursing in his veins.

205 Gordafaríd, when she could see Sohráb

Was racing toward her like a raging flame,

کمان بزه را ببازو فگند

سمندش برآمد بابر بلند

سر نیزه را سوی سهراب کرد

عنان و سنان را پر از تاب کرد

برآشفت سهراب و شد چون پلنگ

چو بدخواه او چاره گر بد بجنگ

عنان بر گرایید وبرگاشت اسپ

بیامد بکردار آذر گشسپ

۲۱۰   ز دوده سنان آنگهی در ربود

درآمد بدو هم بکردار دود

بزد بر کمربند گرد آفرید

زره بر برش یک بیک بر درید

ز زین بر گرفتش بکردار گوی

چو چوگان بزخم اندر آید بدوی

چو بر زین بپیچید گرد آفرید

یکی تیغ تیز از میان برکشید

بزد نیزهٔ او بدو نیم کرد

نشست از براسپ و برخاست گرد

۲۱۵   به آورد با او بسنده نبود

بپیچید ازو روی و برگاشت زود

سپهبد عنان اژدها را سپرد

بخشم از جهان روشنایی ببرد

چو آمد خروشان بتنگ اندرش

بجنبید وبرداشت خود از سرش

She fixed the bow she'd strung upon her arm;

Her yellow steed reared up to paw the clouds.

She turned her lance's point toward Sohráb,

And then reined in her steed to face her foe.

Sohráb, as fierce as any leopard, had,

Just like his foe, prepared himself to fight.

He turned the reins and brought his horse around,

Then set upon her like the God of Fire.[13]

210 He thrust away her polished lance's point,

And closed upon her like a cloud of smoke.

He struck Gordafaríd upon the waist,

Splitting one by one her armor's links.

Then like a mallet when it strikes the ball,

He drove her from her saddle with one blow.

Gordafaríd, as she was turning in

Her saddle, drew a sharp blade from her waist,

Struck at his lance, and parted it in two,

Then fell back in her seat, dust rising up.

215 She saw she was no match for him in war,

So quickly turned away from him, and fled.

Sohráb then gave his dragon steed its head.

His anger robbed the world of all its light.

As he approached her roaring in his wrath,

She swiftly snatched the helmet from her head,

رها شد ز بند زره موی اوی

درفشان چو خورشید شد روی اوی

بدانست سهراب کو دخترست

سر و موی او از در افسرست

۲۲۰   شگفت آمدش گفت از ایران سپاه

چنین دختر آید به آوردگاه

سواران جنگی بروز نبرد

همانا بابر اندر آرند گرد

زفتراک بگشاد پیچان کمند

بینداخت و آمد میانش ببند

بدو گفت کز من رهایی مجوی

چرا جنگ جویی تو ای ماه روی

نیامد بدامم بسان تو گور

ز چنگم رهایی نیابی مشور

۲۲۵   بدانست کاویخت گردآفرید

مر آنرا جز از چاره درمان ندید

بدو روی بنمود وگفت ای دلیر

میان دلیران بکردار شیر

دو لشکر نظاره برین جنگ ما

برین گرز و شمشیر و آهنگ ما

کنون من گشایم چنین روی وموی

سپاه تو گردد پراز گفت وگوی

که با دختری او بدشت نبرد

بدین سان بابر اندر آورد گرد

Her hair was freed of its heavy armored cloak;

Her face shone forth as radiant as the sun.

Sohráb realized this champion was a maid

Whose face was worthy of a royal crown.

220 He spoke in awe, "From among the army of

Irán a maid like this comes forth, and fights

With mounted warriors in the field of war,

And raises the dust of battle to the sky! "

He loosed his twisted lasso from its loop,

And threw it, catching her around the waist.

Sohráb spoke to her and said, "Don't seek to flee.

Oh beauteous moon, why do you wish to fight?

I've never caught an onager like you.

You'll not escape my grip. Don't even try."

225 Gordafaríd knew that she was caught at last.

She could not free herself, save through some trick.

She turned her face to him and said, "Oh, brave

And peerless youth, so like a lion when

You face your foe, two armies watch our fight,

Our combat here of heavy mace and blade.

Should I reveal to them my face and hair,

Your army will be filled with murmuring.

'Sohráb in battle with a maiden foe,

Labored so hard that dust rose up in clouds.'

۲۳۰ نهانی بسازیم بهتر بود

خرد داشتن کار مهتر بود

ز بهر من آهو ز هر سو مخواه

میان دو صف بر کشیده سپاه

کنون لشکر و دژ بفرمان تست

نباید برین آشتی جنگ جست

دژ و گنج و دژبان سراسر تراست

چو آیی بدان ساز کت دل هواست

چو رخساره بنمود سهراب را

ز خوشاب بگشاد عناب را

۲۳۵ یکی بوستان بد در اندر بهشت

ببالای او سرو دهقان نکشت

دو چشمش گوزن و دو ابرو کمان

تو گفتی همی بشکفد هر زمان

ز گفتار او مبتلا شد دلش

برافروخت و گنج بلا شد دلش

بدو گفت کاکنون ازین بر مگرد

که دیدی مرا روزگار نبرد

برین بارهٔ دژ دل اندر مبند

که این نیست برتر ز ابر بلند

۲۴۰ بپای آورد زخم کوپال من

نراند کسی نیزه بر یال من

عنان را بپیچید گرد آفرید

سمند سرافراز بر دژ کشید

230 To parley here in secret would be best.

A noble man must use his head as well.

Do not bring shame upon yourself before

These two ranked armies here because of me.

You now command the garrison and fort.

Why should you now make war instead of peace?

Once you accept this treaty which you wish,

The fort, its chief and treasure are all yours."

She turned her face and smiled upon Sohráb,

Showing him her pearly teeth and ruby lips.

235 She seemed a garden fair as paradise.

No gardener's seen so tall a cypress tree.

Her eyes were like a deer's, her eyebrows bows.

She seemed a flower in the height of bloom.

These words of hers perplexed Sohráb at heart.

His cheeks grew flaming hot, his thoughts confused.

He said to her, "Do not betray your word—

You've faced me on the field of battle once—

Nor fix your hopes on these high fortress walls.

They are not higher than the clouds above.

240 My mace's blows will bring them to the ground,

And there's no lance that will ever pierce my chest."

Gordafaríd pulled at her horse's reins,

Turning her yellow steed toward the fort.

همی رفت وسهراب بااو بهم

بیامد بدرگاه دژ گژدهم

درباره بگشاد گرد آفرید

تن خسته و بسته بر دژ کشید

در دژ ببستند و غمگین شدند

پر از غم دل ودیده خونین شدند

۲۴۵   ز آزار گردآفرید و هجیر

پر از درد بودند برنا وپیر

بگفتند کای نیکدل شیرزن

پر از غم بد از تو دل انجمن

که هم رزم جستی هم افسون و رنگ

نیامد ز کار تو بر دوده ننگ

بخندید بسیار گرد آفرید

بباره برآمد سپه بنگرید

چو سهراب را دید بر پشت زین

چنین گفت کای شاه ترکان چین

۲۵۰   چرا رنجه گشتی کنون باز گرد

هم از آمدن هم ز دشت نبرد

بخندید و او را به افسوس گفت

که ترکان ز ایران نیابند جفت

چنین بود و روزی نبودت ز من

بدین درد غمگین مکن خویشتن

همانا که تو خود ز ترکان نۀ

که جز بافرین بزرگان نۀ

She rode along; Sohráb was at her side,

Old Gazhdahám watched from the battlements.

Gordafaríd swung wide the fortress gate,

And drew her bound and weary body through.

They sadly closed the gate behind her then.

Their hearts were filled with grief, their eyes with tears.

245 Her grievous wounds and those of brave Hojír,

Had saddened all within, both young and old.

"Oh brave and lion-hearted maid," they said,

"The hearts of all are mournful at your state.

You have fought well, and tried deceit and guile.

Your deeds have brought no shame upon your line."

Gordafaríd laughed loud and long, then climbed

The fortress wall to look upon their foes.

She saw Sohráb still seated on his mount,

And called, "Oh shah who leads the Chinese Turks,

250 Why strive so hard? Turn back from this attack,

And from all combat on the field of war.

She laughed once more and spoke in mockery,

"The Turks will find no mates within Irán;

That's how it is, you had no luck with me.

But don't distress yourself too much at that.

You're surely not descended from these Turks.

You must be born of some more noble race.

بدان زور وبازوی و آن کتف ویال

نداری کس از پهلوانان همال

۲۵۵   ولیکن چو آگاهی آید بشاه

که آورد گردی ز توران سپاه

شهنشاه و رستم بجنبد ز جای

شما با تهمتن ندارید پای

نماند یکی زنده از لشکرت

ندانم چه آید ز بد برسرت

دریغ آیدم کین چنین یال وسفت

همی از پلنگان بباید نهفت

ترا بهتر آید که فرمان کنی

رخ نامور سوی توران کنی

۲۶۰   نباشی بس ایمن ببازوی خویش

خورد گاو نادان ز پهلوی خویش

چو بشنید سهراب ننگ آمدش

که آسان همی دژ بچنگ آمدش

بزیر دژ اندر یکی جای بود

کجا دژ بدان جای بر پای بود

بتاراج داد آن همه بوم ورست

بیکبارگی دست بد را بشست

چنین گفت کامروز بیگاه گشت

ز پیگار مان دست کوتاه گشت

۲۶۵   برآرم بشبگیر ازین باره گرد

به بیند آسیب روز نبرد

With your great strength of arm, your chest and neck,

None of these *pahlaváns* can equal you.

255 However when Shah Kay Kavús learns that

Some warrior's brought an army from Turán,

He'll tell Rostám to arm himself for war.

Rostam's a hero you can never match.

Of all your host he'll leave not one alive.

And I cannot guess what evil you'll endure.

I'm saddened that a chest and neck like yours

Should disappear within some leopard's maw.

It's better if you heed my warning now,

And turn your noble face toward Turán.

260 Don't trust your arm alone. The foolish bull

Will only feed, and think not of the knife."

Sohráb felt shame at what he heard. The fort

Had come so easily within his grasp.

Around the citadel there lay a settlement,

A town and fields, in which the fortress stood.

He razed the town and burned the fields,

Abandoning himself to evil deeds.

Sohráb asserted, "The day's come to an end;

Our hands are stayed from battle now by night.

265 At dawn tomorrow I'll pull down these walls;

They too shall look upon defeat in war."

چو برگشت سهراب گژدهم پیر

بیاورد وبنشاند مردی دبیر

یکی نامه بنوشت نزدیک شاه

برافگند پوینده مردی براه

نخست آفرین کرد بر کردگار

نمود آنگهی گردش روزگار

که آمد برما سپاهی گران

همه رزم جویان کندآوران

۲۷۰   یکی پهلوانی بپیش اندرون

که سالش ده و دو نباشد فزون

ببالا ز سرو سهی برترست

چو خورشید تابان بدو پیکرست

برش چون بر پیل وبالاش برز

ندیدم کسی را چنان دست وگرز

چو شمشیر هندی بچنگ آیدش

ز دریا و از کوه تنگ آیدش

چو آواز او رعد غرّنده نیست

چو بازوی او تیغ برّنده نیست

۲۷۵   هجیر دلاور میانرا ببست

یکی بارهٔ تیزتگ بر نشست

بشد پیش سهراب رزم آزمای

بر اسپش ندیدم فزون زان پای

که برهم زند مژه را جنگ جوی

§*Gazhdahám's Letter to Kay Kavús*

When Sohráb had gone, old Gazhdahám, the wise,

Sent for a scribe and sat him by his side.

He swiftly wrote a letter to the shah,

And sent a courier galloping on his way.

At first he praised the Maker of the World,

And next recounted what he'd heard and seen.

"*A mighty host is camped before our walls,*

An army filled with fierce and warlike men.

270 *Their leader is a youthful pahlaván*

Whose years cannot be more than twelve.

His stature exceeds by far a cypress tree's;

His countenance is like the burning sun's.

His chest is like an elephant's, and I

Have never seen a fist and mace like his.

When he takes his Indian sword in hand,

To fight with sea and mountains shames his skill.

The morning thunder cannot match his voice.

The cutting sword cannot withstand his arm.

275 *The brave Hojír prepared himself for war,*

And mounted on a swift-paced horse, he went

To fight Sohráb, for that's this hero's name.

I did not see him on his horse for longer

Than it takes a warrior to knit his brows,

گراید ز بینی سوی مغز بوی

که سهرابش از پشت زین برگرفت

برش ماند زان بازو اندر شگفت

درستست و اکنون بزنهار اوست

پر اندیشه جان از پی کار اوست

۲۸۰   سواران ترکان بسی دیده ام

عنان پیچ زین گونه نشنیده ام

مبادا که او درمیان دو صف

یکی مرد جنگ آور آرد بکف

بران کوه بخشایش آرد زمین

که او اسپ تازد برو روز کین

عنان دار چون او ندیدست کس

تو گفتی که سام سوارست وبس

بلندیش برآسمان رفته گیر

سر بخت گردان همه خفته گیر

۲۸۵   اگر خود شکیبیم یک چند نیز

نکوشیم و دیگر نگوییم چیز

اگر دم زند شهریار زمین

نراند سپاه ونسازد کمین

دژ وباره گیرد که خود زور هست

نگیرد کسی دست اورا بدست

که این باره را نیست پایاب اوی

درنگی شود شیر ز اشتاب اوی

Or for a scent to move from nose to brain.

Sohráb unhorsed him with a single blow,

His chest astonished by that fearful arm.

He's still alive, although his prisoner.

Our souls are filled with anguish at his state.

280 *Many a Turkish horseman have I known;*

I've never seen or heard of one like this.

God grant no warrior of ours should ever

Fight with him before two armies' ranks.

Should he assault a mountain in his wrath,

The earth itself would pity stone and flint.

No one has seen a cavalier like him;

You'd think he was the horseman Sam, no less.

His height, take it as reaching to the sky.

And take our heroes' luck as slumbering.

285 *Should we ourselves delay now for a while,*

And neither do nor say what must be done;

Or if the shahansháh should pause to breathe;

And neither sends an army nor prepares

To fight, he'll seize both fort and barricade.

He has the strength. No one can stay his hand.

This fortress wall cannot withstand his might.

The lion's charge seems slow before his speed.

چو نامه بمهر اندر آمد بشب

فرستاده را جست و بگشاد لب

۲۹۰   فرستاد نامه سوی راه راست

پس نامه آنگاه بر پای خاست

بنه برنهاد وسراندر کشید

بران راه بی راه شد ناپدید

سوی شهر ایران نهادند روی

سپردند آن بارهٔ دژ بدوی

چو خورشید برزد سراز تیره کوه

میانرا ببستند ترکان گروه

سپهدار سهراب نیزه بدست

یکی بارکش بارهٔ بر نشست

۲۹۵   سوی باره آمد یکی بنگرید

بباره درون بس کسی را ندید

بیامد در دژ گشادند باز

ندیدند در دژ یکی رزمساز

بفرمان همه پیش او آمدند

بجان هرکسی چاره جو آمدند

چو نامه بنزدیک خسرو رسید

غمی شد دلش کان سخنها شنید

گرانمایگانرا ز لشکر بخواند

وزین داستان چند گونه براند

۳۰۰   نشستند باشاه ایران بهم

And when the letter had been sealed that night,

He called a messenger and spoke to him.

290   He sent his letter by the straightest route,

When that was done, Gazhdám rose up and left.

The rider seized his bag, put down his head,

And disappeared along untraveled ways.

The others turned their faces toward Irán,

Abandoning the fortress to Sohráb.

When dawn appeared above the mountain peaks,

The Turkish forces armed themselves for war.

Sohráb, the army's marshal, lance in hand,

And seated on a heavy-shouldered steed,

295   Approached the fortress walls and looked inside,

But there were few within to meet his gaze.

As he advanced they swung the portal wide,

But in the fort he saw not one to fight.

Those left within approached at his command,

Each thinking how he might escape his wrath.

§*Kay Kavús*

When this report was brought to Kay Kavús,

The words of Gazhdahám dismayed his heart.

He called the army's leaders to his side,

And spoke at length of his account with them.

300   The army's chiefs, both great and small, men like

بزرگان لشکر همه بیش وکم

چو طوس وچو گودرز کشواد وگیو

چو گرگین وبهرام و فرهاد نیو

سپهدار نامه برایشان بخواند

بپرسید بسیار وخیره بماند

چنین گفت با پهلوانان براز

که این کار گردد بما بر دراز

برین سان که گژدهم گوید همی

از اندیشه دلرا بشوید همی

۳۰۵ چه سازیم و درمان این کار چیست

از ایران هم آورد این مرد کیست

بر آن برنهادند یکسر که گیو

بزابل شود نزد سالار نیو

نشست آنگهی رای زد با دبیر

که کاری گزاینده بد ناگزیر

یکی نامه فرمود پس شهریار

نوشتن بر رستم نامدار

نخست آفرین کرد بر کردگار

جهاندار و پروردۀ روزگار

۳۱۰ دگر آفرین کرد بر پهلوان

که بیدار دل باش و روشن روان

دل و پشت گردان ایران تویی

بچنگال ونیروی شیران تویی

گشایندۀ بند هاماوران

Gudárz of Keshvád's house, like Tus and Giv,

Like Bahram and Gorgín, and like Farhád,

Sat down to take their counsel with the shah.

He read the letter for them all, and spoke

Of his distress and grave perplexity.

He spoke in privacy to all his chiefs,

"I fear this matter won't be settled soon.

Gazhdáhm's report of how this matter stands

Has driven other thoughts out of my mind.

305 What can we do, where lies the remedy?

In all Irán what warrior's his match?"

They all agreed that Giv should leave at once

To seek the martial chieftan of Zaból.[14]

The shah sent for his minister at once;

This was a matter of great urgency.

When they'd conferred he ordered him to write

A letter to the world-renowned Rostám.

He praised the Maker of the World at first,

Him who created all, and shapes our Fate.

310 And then he praised the noble *pahlaván*.

"Be vigilant of heart and of bright soul.

You are the spine and heart of all our chiefs—

A lion in ferocity and strength.

You freed the captives of Hamavarán,

ستانندهٔ مرز مازندران

ز گرز تو خورشید گریان شود

ز تیغ تو ناهید بریان شود

چو گرد پی رخش تو نیل نیست

هم آورد تو درجهان پیل نیست

۳۱۵   کمند تو بر شیر بند افگند

سنان تو کوهی ز بن برکند

تویی از همه بد بایران پناه

ز تو برفرازند گردان کلاه

گزاینده کاری بد آمد بپیش

کز اندیشهٔ آن دلم گشت ریش

نشستند گردان بپیشم بهم

چو خواندیم آن نامهٔ گژدهم

چنان باد کاندر جهان جز توکس

نباشد بهر کار فریادرس

۳۲۰   بدان گونه دیدند گردان نیو

که پیش تو آید گرانمایه گیو

چو نامه بخوانی بروز وبشب

مکن داستان را گشاده دولب

مگر با سواران بسیار هوش

ز زابل برانی برآری خروش

بر اینسان که گژدهم زو یاد کرد

نباید جز از تو ورا هم نبرد

بگیو آنگهی گفت برسان دود

You seized the region of Mazandarán.[15]

The sun itself weeps at your heavy mace.

Your bright blade singes Nahíd's brow.[16]

No indigo's so dark as Rakhsh's dust.

No elephant's so fierce as you in war.

315   *Your lasso binds the lion on the plain;*

    Your spear uproots the mountain from the earth.

    You are the refuge of Irán from every ill.

    You are the diadem in all our crowns.

    An urgent, fearful threat confronts us now,

    The very thought of which has pierced my heart.

    The heroes of Irán have counseled me,

    As we read Gazhdahám's account, and we've

    Concluded that in all the world there's none

    Save you who triumphs over every foe.

320   *Since that's the case, our noble chieftans saw*

    That worthy Giv should hasten to your court.

    When you have read these words, whether it be day

    Or night, don't open your mouth to speak of it,

    Unless to raise the battle cry and lead

    Your horsemen galloping from Zabol's gates.

    As Gazhdahám describes Sohráb, you are

    His only equal on the battlefield.

    The shah then ordered Giv, "Now you must seize

عنان تگاور بباید بسود

۳۲۵   بباید که نزدیک رستم شوی

بزابل نمانی وگر نغنوی

اگر شب رسی روز را بازگرد

بگویش که تنگ اندر آمد نبرد

ازو نامه بستد بکردار آب

برفت و نجست ایچ آرام و خواب

چو نزدیکی زابلستان رسید

خروش طلایه بدستان رسید

تهمتن پذیره شدش باسپاه

نهادند برسر بزرگان کلاه

۳۳۰   پیاده شدش گیو وگردان بهم

هر آنکس که بودند از بیش و کم

ز اسپ اندر آمد گو نامدار

از ایران بپرسید وز شهریار

ز ره سوی ایوان رستم شدند

ببودند یکبار و دم برزدند

بگفت آنچ بشنید و نامه بداد

ز سهراب چندی سخن کرد یاد

تهمتن چو بشنید ونامه بخواند

بخندید وزان کار خیره بماند

۳۳۵   که مانندهٔ سام گرد از مهان

سواری پدید آمد اندر جهان

از آزادگان این نباشد شگفت

Your horse's reins and gallop swift as smoke.

325 Proceed at once to brave Rostám, but in

Zaból don't pause to rest or think of sleep.

If you arrive by night, return at dawn.

Tell him the battle presses at our door."

He took the letter from his hand and rode,

Swift as a stream, and neither paused nor slept.

As Giv approached Zabolestán, the cries

Of his patrols brought word of this to Zal.[17]

Rostám rode out to greet him with his troops,

The leaders dressed in crowns and robes of state.

330 Then all dismounted from their steeds as one,

The nobles great and small, and Giv as well.

Rostám approached him then on foot, and asked

His news of both Irán and Shah Kavús.

They left the road to seek the royal court,

And rested there a while, and drew their breath.

Giv told him all he'd heard, and gave

Rostám the letter from the shah. He spoke

About Sohráb as well. When he was done,

The lord of Zabol laughed aloud and said,

335 "A noble warrior has now appeared

Who is the equal of the hero Sam.

Were he Iranian this might be so.

ز ترکان چنین یاد نتوان گرفت

من از دخت شاه سمنگان یکی

پسر دارم و باشد او کودکی

هنوز آن گرامی نداند که جنگ

توان کرد باید گه نام و ننگ

فرستادمش زرّ و گوهر بسی

بر مادر او بدست کسی

۳۴۰   چنین پاسخ آمد که آن ارجمند

بسی بر نیاید که گردد بلند

همی می خورد بالب شیربوی

شود بی گمان زود پرخاشجوی

بباشیم یکروز و دم برزنیم

یکی بر لب خشک نم برزنیم

ازان پس گراییم نزدیک شاه

بگردان ایران نماییم راه

مگر بخت رخشنده بیدار نیست

وگرنه چنین کار دشوار نیست

۳۴۵   چو دریا بموج اندرآید زجای

ندارد دم آتش تیز پای

درفش مرا چون ببیند ز دور

دلش ماتم آرد بهنگام سور

بدین تیزی اندر نیاید بجنگ

نباید گرفتن چنین کار تنگ

بمی دست بردند و مستان شدند

But from the Turks it cannot be believed.

I have a son by princess Tahminé

Of Semengán, but he is still a child.

That precious infant's not yet learned a man

Must fight to keep his name and honor pure.

I sent a message to his mother once

With many jewels, and golden coins as well.

340   She answered me, 'This precious boy is still

A child, although he'll soon be tall and strong.

He drinks his wine with lips that smell of milk,

Though doubtless he'll grow fierce and warlike soon.'

Let's stay one day, and so refresh ourselves.

Our lips are dry, let's moisten them with wine.

And after that, we'll hasten to the shah,

And lead the heroes of Irán to war.

It may be that our shining fortune sleeps.

If not, such matters are not difficult.

345   For when the ocean rises up in waves,

The fiercest flame cannot resist it long.

My banner, when he spies it from afar,

Will turn his victory feast into a wake.

I doubt that he'll be eager then to fight.

This is no threat to trouble hearts like ours."

They called for wine, first toasted Kay Kavús

ز یاد سپهبد بدستان شدند

دگر روز شبگیر هم پر خمار

بیامد تهمتن برآراست کار

۳۵۰ ز مستی هم آن روز باز ایستاد

دوم روز رفتن نیامدش یاد

سه دیگر سحرگه بیاورد می

نیامد ورا یاد کاوس کی

بروز چهارم برآراست گیو

چنین گفت با گرد سالار نیو

که کاوس تندست و هشیار نیست

هم این داستان بردلش خوار نیست

غمی بود ازین کار و دل پر شتاب

شده دور ازو خورد و آرام وخواب

۳۵۵ بزابلستان گر درنگ آوریم

زمی باز پیگار و جنگ آوریم

بدو گفت رستم که مندیش ازین

که باما نشورد کس اندر زمین

بفرمود تا رخش را زین کنند

دم اندر دم نای روئین کنند

سواران زابل شنیدند نای

برفتند با ترگ و جوشن ز جای

گُرازان بدرگاه شاه آمدند

گشاده دل و نیک خواه آمدند

And then Dastán, then drank the whole day through,

The next day just at dawn, Rostám appeared,

Still dazed with drink, and called again for wine.

350 They drank away that second day as well,

Nor did they give a thought to their return.

And on the third, when they brought wine at dawn,

No thought of Kay Kavús came to his mind.

But on the fourth, the noble Giv prepared

Himself to leave and pleaded with Rostám,

"Kavús is quick of temper and not shrewd,

And this affair's a burden on his mind.

It's vexed his soul and sorely pained his heart.

He neither eats nor sleeps nor takes his ease.

355 Should we delay here longer in Zaból,

We'll draw this strife and turmoil to Irán."

Rostám replied, "Be easy in your mind.

There's none who dares to turn his wrath on me."

He had them saddle Rakhsh with greatest speed,

And ordered them to sound the brazen horns.

The horsemen of Zaból heard this alarm,

And swiftly left their homes with shields and arms.

§*Rostám at Court*

They galloped toward the court of Shah Kavús,

With loyal thoughts and open hearts they came.

۳۶۰ چو رفتند و بردند پیشش نماز

برآشفت و پاسخ نداد ایچ باز

یکی بانگ برزد بگیو از نخست

پس آنگاه شرم از دو دیده بشست

که رستم که باشد که فرمان من

کند پست و پیچد ز پیمان من

بگیر و ببر زنده بردار کن

وزو نیز بامن مگردان سخن

ز گفتار او گیو را دل بخست

که بردی برستم بران گونه دست

۳۶۵ برآشفت با گیو وباپیلتن

فرو ماند خیره همه انجمن

بفرمود پس طوس را شهریار

که رو هردو رازنده برکن بدار

خود از جای برخاست کاوس کی

برافروخت بر سان آتش زنی

بشد طوس و دست تهمتن گرفت

بدو مانده پرخاش جویان شگفت

که از پیش کاوس بیرون بَرد

مگر کاندر آن تیزی افسون برد

۳۷۰ تهمتن برآشفت با شهریار

که چندین مدار آتش اندرکنار

همه کارت از یکدیگر بدترست

360 But when they entered and bowed low to him,

Kavús grew angry, and answered not a word.

At first he shouted once, at noble Giv,

Then washed his eyes quite free of shame.

"Who is Rostám to turn his back to me,

And give so little heed to my command?

Seize him, take him from here, and gibbet him

Alive. Then speak no more of him to me!"

Giv's heart was torn asunder by these words.

"Will you indeed mistreat Rostám like this?"

365 When he grew angry with Piltán and Giv,[18]

Those gathered in the court were thunderstruck.

The shah commanded Tus as he stood there.

"Go now and hang the both of them alive!"

The shah himself rose up from his high throne,

His anger flaring up like flames from reeds,

As Tus approached Rostám and seized his arm

The warriors there could not believe their eyes.

Did he intend to march him from the court?

Or did his brusqueness mask a shrewd deceit?

370   Tahamtán in turn grew angry with the shah.

"Don't nurse so hot a fire within your breast.

Each thing you do shames that already done.

ترا شهریاری نه اندر خورست

تو سهراب را زنده بردار کن

پر آشوب و بدخواه را خوارکن

بزد تند یک دست بر دست طوس

تو گفتی ز پیل ژیان یافت کوس

ز بالا نگون اندر آمد بسر

برو کرد رستم بتندی گذر

۳۷۵   بدر شد بخشم اندر آمد برَخش

منم گفت شیر اوژن و تاج بخش

چو خشم آورم شاه کاؤس کیست

چرا دست یازد بمن طوس کیست

زمین بنده و رخش گاه منست

نگین گرز و مِغفر کلاه منست

شب تیره از تیغ رخشان کنم

به آوردگه بر سر افشان کنم

سرنیزه و تیغ یار من اند

دوبازو و دل شهریار من اند

۳۸۰   چه آزاردم او و نه من بنده ام

یکی بندهٔ آفریننده ام

بایران ار ایدونکه سهراب گرد

بیاید نماند بزرگ و نه خرد

شما هرکسی چارهٔ جان کنید

خرد را بدین کار پیچان کنید

بایران نبینید ازین پس مرا

You are unworthy of both throne and rule.

You go and hang the brave Sohráb alive!

Take arms, set forth and humble him yourself!"

Rostám struck Tus's hand a single blow,

But like that of a raging elephant,

And sent that worthy sprawling on the ground.

Rostám passed by him then with rapid strides,

375 Went out the door and mounted Rakhsh. "I am,"

He said, "the lion-heart who gave this crown."[19]

When I'm enraged, who then is Shah Kavús?

Who's there to humble me? Who is this Tus?

The earth's my servant and my throne is Rakhsh;

This mace my signet ring, this helm my crown.

My sword illuminates the darkest night,

And scatters heads upon the battlefield.

My comrades are this spear and shining blade;

My heart and these two arms my only shah.

380 How dare he order me! I'm not his slave.

I serve the World Creator, only Him.

If this Sohráb should now invade Irán,

There's none who will be spared, not great nor small.

You all must seek some way to save your souls.

You all must bend your wisdom to that task.

You'll see Rostám no more within Irán.

شما را زمین پـَرّ کَرگَـس مرا

غمی شد دل نامداران همه

که رستم شبان بود و ایشان رمه

۳۸۵   بگودرز گفتند کین کارتست

شکسته بدست تو گردد درست

سپهبد جز از تو سخن نشنود

همی بخت تو زین سخن نغنود

بنزدیک این شاه دیوانه رو

وزین در سخن یاد کن نوبنو

سخنهای چرب و دراز آوری

مگر بخت گم بوده باز آوری

سپهدار گودرز کشواد رفت

بنزدیک خسرو خرامید تفت

۳۹۰   بکاوس کی گفت رستم چه کرد

کز ایران برآوردی امروز گَـرد

چو او رفت و آمد سپاهی بزرگ

یکی پهلوانی بکردار گرگ

که داری که بااو بدشت نبرد

شود بر فشاند برو تیره گرد

یلان ترا سر بسر گژدهم

شنیدست و دیدست از بیش وکم

همی گوید آن روز هرگز مباد

که بااو سواری کند رزم یاد

۳۹۵   کسی را که جنگی چو رستم بود

You have the land, I fly on vultures' wings."[20]

The hearts of all the notables were sad.

Their shepherd was Rostám, and they the flock.

385 They sought Gudárz, "This is a task for you.

What's broken will be mended in your hand.

Shah Kay Kavús will hear no speech but yours,[21]

Nor will our fortune slumber at your words.

Approach this crazed and foolish shah at once,

And speak with him anew of what's just passed.

If you speak shrewdly and at length, you may

Regain the smiling fortune we have lost."

The *sepahdár* Gudárz, Keshvád's brave son,

Rode swiftly off to court, and to the shah.

390 He asked Kavús, "What can Rostám have done

That you would cast Irán into the dust?

When he is gone, an army will attack,

Led by that wolflike *pahlaván*, Sohráb.

Who's there to equal him upon the field

Of war? Who'll heap dark dust upon his head?

Your warriors, both great and small, are known

To Gazhdahám, he's seen and heard them all.

He says, 'I pray the day may never come

That one of us must challenge him.'

395 Whoever has a champion like Rostám,

بیازارد اورا خرد کم بود

چو بشنید گفتار گودرز شاه

بدانست کو دارد آیین و راه

پشیمان بشد زان کجا گفته بود

ببیهودگی مغزش آشفته بود

بگودرز گفت این سخن درخورست

لب پیر با پند نیکوترست

خردمند باید دل پادشا

که تیزی و تندی نیارد بها

۴۰۰   شما را بباید بر او شدن

بخوبی بسی داستانها زدن

سرش کردن از تیزی من تهی

نمودن بدو روزگار بهی

چو گودرز برخاست از پیش اوی

پس پهلوان تیز بنهاد روی

برفتند باو سران سپاه

پس رستم اندر گرفتند راه

چو دیدند گرد گو پیلتن

همه نامداران شدند انجمن

۴۰۵   ستایش گرفتند بر پهلوان

که جاوید بادی و روشن روان

جهان سربسر زیر پای توباد

همیشه سرتخت جای تو باد

تو دانی که کاؤس را مغز نیست

And drives him from the court, has little sense."

When Kay Kavús had heard the counsel of

Gudárz, he realized he spoke the truth.

He was ashamed of everything he'd said.

His wits had been confused by fear and wrath.

"Your speech is to the point," he told Gudárz.

"Advice sits well upon an old man's lips.

A padisháh should be more wise of speech,

For anger and quick words bring no reward.

400   You must now hasten to the brave Rostám

And speak with him at length and counsel him.

Make him forget this hastiness of mine.

Recall to him the thoughts of better times."

Gudárz rose up and left the royal court,

Then galloped swiftly off toward Rostám.

The army's leaders joined him on the road,

And followed in the tracks of Tahamtán.

When they could see the dust that hero raised,

The lords and notables all gathered to

405   His side. They praised the *pahlaván* and said,

"Be of bright soul and live forever young.

May all the world be ever at your feet,

And may you sit forever on a throne.

You know Kavús, he has no brains at all.

بتیزی سخن گفتنش نغز نیست

بجوشد همانگه پشیمان شود

بخوبی ز سر باز پیمان شود

تهمتن گر آزرده گردد ز شاه

هم ایرانیانرا نباشد گناه

۴۱۰   هم او زان سخنها پشیمان شدست

ز تندی بخاید همی پشت دست

تهمتن چنین پاسخ آورد باز

که هستم ز کاوس کی بی نیاز

مرا تخت زین باشد و تاج ترگ

قبا جوشن و دل نهاده بمرگ

چرا دارم از خشم کاوس باک

چه کاوس پیشم چه یک مشت خاک

سرم گشت سیر و دلم کرد بس

جز از پاک یزدان نترسم ز کس

۴۱۵   ز گفتار چون سیر گشت انجمن

چنین گفت گودرز با پیلتن

که شهر و دلیران و لشکر گمان

بدیگر سخنها برند این زمان

کزین ترک ترسنده شد سرفراز

همی رفت زین گونه چندی براز

که چونان که گژدهم داد آگهی

همه بوم و بر کرد باید تهی

چو رستم همی زو بترسد بجنگ

He speaks too hastily, and that's not good.

He'll boil up in a flash, then be ashamed,

And meekly seek to mend his bonds anew.

If Tahamtán is angry with the shah,

The people of Irán have done no wrong.

410 The shah himself regrets his words and bites

The knuckles of his hand in range and shame."

The brave Rostám replied to them in turn,

"I have no need of Kay Kavús, not I.

This saddle is my throne, this helm my crown.

Chainmail's my robe; my heart's prepared for death.

Why should I fear the anger of Kavús?

The shah's no more to me than is this dirt.

My head's grown weary, and my heart is full.

Besides Yazdán the Pure, whom should I fear?"[22]

415 When they had had their fill of his reply,

Gudárz spoke bluntly with Piltán and said,

"The shah, the nobles and the army all

Will see your actions in another light.

Our noble lord grew fearful of this Turk,

And thus departed secretly from here.

Since Gazhdahám has warned us of Sohráb,

We must abandon all Irán at once.

When brave Rostám flees from the battlefield,

مرا و ترا نیست جای درنگ

۴۲۰ از آشفتن شاه وپیگار اوی

بدیدم بدرگاه بر گفت وگوی

ز سهراب یل رفت یکسر سخن

چنین پشت برشاه ایران مکن

چنین برشده نامت اندر جهان

بدین باز گشتن مَگردان نهان

و دیگر که تنگ اندر آمد سپاه

مکن تیره برخیره این تاج وگاه

برستم بر این داستانها بخواند

تهمتن چو بشنید خیره بماند

۴۲۵ بدو گفت اگر بیم دارد دلم

نخواهم که باشد ز تن بُگسِلم

ازین ننگ برگشت وآمد براه

گرازان وپویان بنزدیک شاه

چو در شد ز در شاه بر پای خاست

بسی پوزش اندر گذشته بخواست

که تندی مرا گوهرست وسرشت

چنان زیست باید که یزدان بکِشت

وزین ناسگالیده بدخواه نو

دلم گشت باریک چون ماه نو

۴۳۰ بدین چاره جستن ترا خواستم

چو دیر آمدی تندی آراستم

چو آزرده گشتی تو ای پیلتن

It's not for you and me to stay and fight.

420 I've heard much comment on Kavús's rage

At court, and of his hasty words and deeds,

But all there speak with wonder of Sohráb.

Don't turn your back upon our royal shah.

Your name has grown renowned throughout the world,

Don't bring it low by turning now to flight.

What's more, the enemy is at our gate.

Do not endanger more this crown and throne."

Gudárz thus spoke his reasons to Rostám,

Who heard them with astonishment and shame.

425 He said, "If fear afflicts my heart, then I've

No use for it. I'll tear it from my chest."

He turned aside from shame, took to the road,

And galloped swiftly back toward the shah.

And when he strode into the court, Kavús

Stood up and asked forgiveness of Rostám.

"I am by nature rash in speech and act,

But one must be as God created him.

This unexpected foe oppressed my heart

Until like the moon, it grew both pale and weak.

430 To find some remedy I sent for you.

When you were slow to come, I grew enraged.

When I saw you were distressed, Piltán, I felt

پشیمان شدم خاکم اندر دهن

بدو گفت رستم که گیهان تراست

همه کهترانیم و فرمان تراست

کنون آمدم تا چه فرمان دهی

روانت ز دانش مبادا تهی

بدو گفت کاؤس کامروز بزم

گزینیم و فردا بسازیم رزم

۴۳۵   بیاراست رامشگهی شاهوار

شد ایوان بکردار باغ بهار

ز آواز ابریشم وبانگ نای

سمن عارضان پیش خسرو بپای

همی باده خوردند تا نیم شب

ز خنیاگران بر گشاده دولب

دگر روز فرمود تا گیو و طوس

ببستند شبگیر بر پیل کوس

در گنج بگشاد و روزی بداد

سپه برنشاند وبنه بر نهاد

۴۴۰   سپردار و جوشنوران صدهزار

شمرده بلشکرگه آمد سوار

یکی لشکر آمد ز پهلو بدشت

که از گرد ایشان هوا تیره گشت

سراپرده و خیمه زد بر دو میل

Remorse, and shame has filled my mouth with dust."

Rostám replied, "Oh, shah, the world is yours.

We are your subjects. Yours is sovereignty.

I've come to court to be at your command.

May the wisdom of your soul be never less."

Kavús replied, "Today let's choose instead

To celebrate. Tomorrow we'll make war."

435 A place was then prepared, fit for a shah;

The palace was adorned like verdant spring.

And there they drank their wine while pale-

Cheeked beauties waited on the shah, and to

The sound of silken strings and plaintive reeds,

The sweet voiced minstrels filled the night with song.

§ *The Iranians Make War*

Next day at dawn he ordered Giv and Tus

To bind the war drums on the elephants.

He opened wide his treasury's doors, gave out

Supplies, and loaded up the baggage train.

440 A hundred thousand men, all bearing shields

And wearing mail, assembled for the march.

From the royal court, an army rode to war

Whose dust rose up and blotted out the sun.

When camped, it spread its tents and canopies

بپوشید گیتی بنعل و بپیل

هوا نیلگون گشت و کوه آبنوس

بجوشید دریا ز آواز کوس

همی رفت منزل بمنزل جهان

شده چون شب و روز گشته نهان

۴۴۵   درخشیدن خشت و ژوپین ز گرد

چو آتش پس پردهٔ لاجورد

ز بس گونه گونه سنان و درفش

سپرهای زرّین و زرّینه کفش

تو گفتی که ابری برنگ آبنوس

برآمد ببارید زو سندروس

جهان را شب و روز پیدا نبود

تو گفتی سپهر و ثریا نبود

ازینسان بشد تا در دژ رسید

بشد خاک و سنگ از جهان ناپدید

۴۵۰   خروشی بلند آمد از دیدگاه

بسهراب گفتند کامد سپاه

چو سهراب زان دیده آوا شنید

بباره بیامد سپه بنگرید

بانگشت لشکر بهومان نمود

سپاهی که آنرا کرانه نبود

چو هومان ز دور آن سپه را بدید

دلش گشت پربیم و دم در کشید

بهومان چنین گفت سهراب گرد

For miles, and carpeted the earth with hooves.

The hills were dark as ebony, the air

Like indigo. The river boiled with drumbeats,

And as the troops proceeded stage by stage,

The world turned dark and night obscured the day.

445   The flash of spears and lances through the dust

Were like bright flames seen through a deep blue haze.

There were so many flags and shining spears,

So many golden shields and gilded boots,

It seemed a cloud as dark as ebony

Had formed, and rained down drops of yellow pitch.

In all the world there was no day or night—

The heavens and Sorayya lost to sight.

So they proceeded to the fortress gates.

The army hid the earth and stones from view.

450   The shouts of lookouts on the fortress walls,

Informed Sohráb the army had arrived.

And when he heard the lookout's cry, Sohráb

Stood on its lofty walls to view his foe.

He showed Humán this vast and fearsome host,

The margins of whose camp could not be seen.

When Humán looked down upon the enemy,

His heart was filled with terror and he groaned.

The brave Sohráb encouraged him, and said,

که اندیشه از دل بباید سترد

۴۵۵ نبینی تو زین لشکر بیکران

یکی مرد جنگی و گرزی گران

که پیش من آید به آوردگاه

گر ایدون که یاری دهد هور وماه

سلیحست بسیار و مردم بسی

سرافراز نامی ندانم کسی

کنون من ببخت رد آفراسیاب

کنم دشت پرخون چو دریای آب

بتنگی نداد ایچ سهراب دل

فرود آمد از باره شاداب دل

۴۶۰ وزانسو سراپردهٔ شهریار

کشیدند بردشت پیش حصار

ز بس خیمه و مرد وپرده سرای

نماند ایچ بر دشت وبرکوه جای

چو خورشید گشت از جهان ناپدید

شب تیره بردشت لشکر کشید

تهمتن بیامد بنزدیک شاه

میان بستهٔ جنگ و دل کینه خواه

که دستور باشد مرا تاجور

از ایدر شوم بی کلاه و کمر

۴۶۵ ببینم که این نوجهاندار کیست

"Relieve your heart of all these fearful thoughts.

455   In all this endless army you'll not see

One warrior, one wielder of the heavy mace,

Who dares approach me on the field of war,

Not even with the aid of sun and moon.

Arms there are in rich array, and many proud

And noble men, all quite unknown to me.

But now, thanks to the great Afrasiyáb,

I'll fill this plain with rivers of their blood."

Sohráb descended lightly from the wall,

His heart untroubled by the thought of war.

460   While on that side, before the fortress walls,

They pitched the royal tents upon the plain.

So many tents and men were gathered there,

No inch of plain or mountain could be seen.

§*Rostám in the Turkish Camp*

When from the earth the sun withdrew its light,

Dark night arrayed its troops upon the field.

Rostám approached the seat of Kay Kavús,

Prepared for war and eager for revenge.

"Let now my monarch's orders be that I

Set out from here with neither helmet nor sword,

465   To spy upon this youthful conqueror,

بزرگان کدامند و سالار کیست

بدو گفت کاؤس کین کارتست

که بیدار دل بادی و تن درست

تهمتن یکی جامهٔ ترکوار

بپوشید و آمد دوان تا حصار

بیامد چو نزدیکی دژ رسید

خروشیدن نوش ترکان شنید

بران دژ درون رفت مرد دلیر

چنانچون سوی آهوان نرّه شیر

۴۷۰   چو سهراب را دید برتخت بزم

نشسته بیک دست او ژنده رزم

بدیگر چو هومان سوار دلیر

دگر بارمان نام‌بردار شیر

تو گفتی همه تخت سهراب بود

بسان یکی سرو شاداب بود

دوبازو بکردار ران هیون

برش چون بر پیل وچهره چو خون

ز ترکان بگرد اندرش صد دلیر

جوان و سرافراز چون نرّه شیر

۴۷۵   پرستار پنجاه با دست بند

بپیش دل افروز تخت بلند

همی یک بیک خواندند آفرین

برآن برز وبالا وتیغ ونگین

همی دید رستم مر او را ز دور

See who his marshal is, and who his chiefs."

Kavús replied, "This is a task for you.

But be alert and guard your safety well."

Rostám put on a costume like the Turks',

And hastened swiftly to the fortress walls.

As Tahamtán approached their camp he heard

The revels of the Turkish troops within.

Then like a lion stalking wild gazelle,

The brave Rostám crept through the fortress gate.

470   He saw Sohráb, enthroned amid the feast,

At his right hand the noble Zhende Razm,

And at his left so brave a horseman as

Humán, and lionlike Barmán as well.

And yet it seemed Sohráb filled up the throne.

His legs and trunk were like a cypress tree;

His arms were heavy as two camels' thighs,

His chest, an elephant's; his face was flushed

With health. A hundred Turkish youths were ranged

Around him there, male lions in their pride.

475   Some fifty servants waited on this high

And happy throne, their wrists adorned with gold.

Each one invoked God's blessing on his sword,

His lofty stature and his signet ring.

While from afar Rostám observed them all—

نشست و نگه کرد مردان سور

بشایسته کاری برون رفت ژند

گوی دید بر سان سرو بلند

بدان لشکر اندر چنو کس نبود

بر رستم آمد بپرسید زود

۴۸۰   چه مردی بدو گفت بامن بگوی

سوی روشنی آی وبنمای روی

تهمتن یکی مشت بر گردنش

بزد تیز و برشد روان از تنش

بدانجایگه خشک شد ژندرزم

نشد ژنده رزم آنگهی سوی بزم

زمانی همی بود سهراب دیر

نیامد بنزدیک او ژند شیر

بپرسید سهراب تا ژند رزم

کجا شد که جایش تهی شد ز بزم

۴۸۵   برفتند و دیدندش افگنده خوار

برآسوده از بزم و از کارزار

خروشان ازان درد باز آمدند

شگفتی فرو مانده از کار ژند

بسهراب گفتند شد ژندرزم

سرآمد برو روز پیگار وبزم

چو بشنید سهراب برجست زود

بیامد بر ژند برسان دود

ابا چاکر و شمع و خنیاگران

These Turkish heroes at their victory feast.

Zhende Razm went out upon some task, and saw

A warrior there, tall as a cypress tree.

Among his troops he knew of none like this.

He moved toward Rostám and challenged him.

480 "Whose man are you?" he asked. "Tell me your name.

Come here, into the light, and show your face! "

Rostám struck Zhende's neck a single blow

That freed his spirit from his body's weight.

He lay upon the ground, now stilled by death.

Brave Zhende Razm returned no more to feast.

After some time had passed, and Zhende Razm

Remained still absent from his side, Sohráb

Inquired about his lion-hearted friend,

"Where did he go? His place is empty here."

485 They went outside and saw him lying there,

Released from feasting and from strife and war.

They all returned lamenting in their pain,

Both anxious and perplexed by Zhende's death.

They told Sohráb, "Brave Zhende Razm is gone,

His days of feasting and of war are done."

Sohráb leapt up on hearing their lament,

Racing swift as smoke to where he lay.

With servants, candles, minstrels in his train,

بیامد ورا دید مرده چنان

۴۹۰ شگفت آمدش سخت و خیره بماند

دلیران و گردنکشان را بخواند

چنین گفت کامشب نباید غنود

همه شب همی نیزه باید بسود

که گرگ اندرآمد میان رمه

سگ و مرد را آزمودش همه

اگر یار باشد جهان آفرین

چو نعل سمندم بساید زمین

ز فتراک زین برگشایم کمند

بخواهم از ایرانیان کین ژند

۴۹۵ بیامد نشست از بر گاه خویش

گرانمایگانرا همه خواند پیش

که گر کم شد از تخت من ژندرزم

نیامد همی سیر جانم ز بزم

چو برگشت رستم بر شهریار

از ایران سپه گیو بد پاسدار

بره بر گو پیلتن را بدید

بزد دست و گرز از میان بر کشید

یکی بر خروشید چون پیل مست

سپر برسر آورد وبنمود دست

۵۰۰ بدانست رستم کز ایران سپاه

بشب گیو باشد طلایه براه

بخندید و زان پس فغان برکشید

He went and looked upon this heavy death.

490   He was amazed, and stood in silent thought,

Then called his brave and gallant *pahlaváns*,

"We must not sleep or rest," he said, "but arm

Ourselves and keep our weapons by our sides.

A wolf has crept within the fold tonight,

Despite the shepherd and his watchful dogs.

But if the World Creator gives me aid

When next my yellow steed tears up the earth,

I'll loose my lasso from its place, and make

Iranians pay the cost of Zhende's death."

495   Sohráb returned and took his seat at court.

Then calling for his notables, he said,

"Though Zhende Razm's place is empty here,

My soul's not wearied yet of reveling."

When bold Rostám returned to seek the shah,

The guard on watch before their camp was Giv.

He saw a man approach who filled the sky.

He grasped his heavy mace and drew it forth.

Then like a maddened elephant he gave

A shout, held up his shield, and challenged him.

500   Rostám, who knew the guardian of

Irán's security that night was Giv,

Laughed once aloud, and then returned a shout.

طلایه چو آواز رستم شنید

بیامد پیاده بنزدیک اوی

چنین گفت کای مهتر جنگجوی

پیاده کجا بودۀ تیره شب

تهمتن بگفتار بگشاد لب

بگفتش بگیو آن کجا کرده بود

چنان شیر مردی که آزرده بود

۵۰۵   وزانجایگه رفت نزدیک شاه

ز ترکان سخن گفت وز بزم گاه

ز سهراب و از برز و بالای اوی

ز بازوی و کتف دلارای اوی

که هرگز ز ترکان چنین کس نخاست

بکردار سروست بالاش راست

بتوران و ایران نماند بکس

تو گوئی که سام سوارست وبس

وزان مشت بر گردن ژندرزم

کزان پس نیامد برزم و ببزم

۵۱۰   بگفتند وپس رود و می خواستند

همه شب همی لشکر آراستند

چو افگند خور سوی بالا کمند

زبانه برآمد ز چرخ بلند

بپوشید سهراب خفتان جنگ

When he had heard the voice of Tahamtán,

Giv rushed to meet him as he neared the lines.

"Oh, noble chief," he said as he approached,

"Where have you been on foot, and in the dark

of night?" Rostám prepared himself to speak.

He told Giv where he'd been and what he'd done,

And that he'd slain a lion-hearted foe.

505   From there he went to see the shah, and told

Him of the Turkish army and their camp,

And of Sohráb's stout arms and mighty chest,

His massive stature and his noble mien.

"No man like him's appeared among the Turks

Before; his stature's like a cypress tree's.

He has no equal here, nor in their camp.

He is the image of the horseman Sam."

He told him how he'd struck brave Zhende Razm,

Who'd go no more to battle or to feast.

510   They spoke awhile, then called for wine and harp.

And all that night the army stood on watch.

§*Sohráb Seeks His Father*

At dawn, when the sun had cast its lasso high,

And tongues of flame shot through the highest sphere,

Sohráb put on his chainmail kaftan lined

نشست از بر چرمهٔ سنگ رنگ

یکی تیغ هندی بچنگ اندرش

یکی مغفر خسروی برسرش

کمندی بفتراک بر شست خم

خم اندر خم و روی کرده دژم

۵۱۵ بیامد یکی برز بالا گزید

بجایی که ایرانیان را بدید

بفرمود تا رفت پیش هجیر

بدو گفت کژی نیاید ز تیر

نشانه نباید که خم آورد

چو پیچان شود زخم کم آورد

بهر کار در پیشه کن راستی

چو خواهی که نگزایدت کاستی

سخن هرچه پرسم همه راست گوی

متاب از ره راستی هیچ روی

۵۲۰ سپارم بتو گنج آراسته

بیابی بسی خلعت و خواسته

ور ایدون که کژی بود رای تو

همان بند و زندان بود جای تو

هجیرش چنین داد پاسخ که شاه

سخن هرچه پرسد ز ایران سپاه

بگویم همه آنچ دانم بدوی

بکژی چرا بایدم گفت و گوی

بدو گفت کز تو بپرسم همه

With silk, and sat upon his silver grey.

He wore a royal helmet on his head,

And in his fist he held an Indian sword.

He fixed his rope in sixty loops upon

The saddle bow, and anger creased his brow.

515 He chose a tower on the wall from which

He might observe the enemy below.

He ordered that Hojír be brought to him,

And warned him, saying, "Try no deceits with me.

A crooked arrow has no use at all.

Unless it's straight no arrow strikes its mark.

In every task you undertake, pursue

The truth, unless you wish to suffer loss.

Whatever I may ask, speak only truth;

Don't deviate at all from right,

520 And I'll reward you with great wealth.

I'll give you precious goods and splendid robes.

But if instead you choose the crooked way,

You'll spend your life in prison and in chains."

Hojír replied, "However he should question me

About the army of Irán, I'll tell

The shah whatever I may know. Why should

I speak dishonestly or bend the truth?"

"I'll question you about the army camped below,"

ز گردنکشان و ز شاه و رمه

۵۲۵   همه نامداران آن مرز را

چو طوس و چو کاوس و گودرز را

ز بهرام واز رستم نامدار

ز هر کت بپرسم بمن بر شمار

بگو کان سراپردۀ هفت رنگ

بدو اندرون خیمه های پلنگ

بپیش اندرون بسته صد ژنده پیل

یکی مهد پیروزه برسان نیل

یکی برز خورشید پیکر درفش

سرش ماه زرّین غلافش بنفش

۵۳۰   بقلب سپاه اندرون جای کیست

ز گردان ایران ورا نام چیست

بدو گفت کان شاه ایران بود

بدرگاه او پیل و شیران بود

وزانپس بدو گفت بر میمنه

سواران بسیار و پیل وبنه

سراپردۀ بر کشیده سیاه

رده گردش اندر ز هر سو سپاه

بگرد اندرش خیمه ز اندازه بیش

پس پشت پیلان و بالاش پیش

۵۳۵   زده پیش او پیل پیکر درفش

بدر بر سواران زرّینه کفش

چنین گفت کان طوس نوذر بود

درفشش کجا پیل پیکر بود

Sohráb then said, "Describe the leaders of

525 Irán to me, its bravest warriors,

Its notables like Tus, Bahrám, Gudárz,

Like Shah Kavús and like far-famed Rostám.

Identify each one I ask of you.

I see a seven-hued pavilion there

Enclosing tents of leopard skin; before

It are a hundred tethered elephants,

A turquoise throne, as dark as indigo;

A banner blazoned with the sun—its case

Is purple and a golden moon surmounts

530 The staff. There, in the army's heart, whose place

Is that, which hero of Irán is he?"

"That is Kavús the shah," Hojír replied,

"His court holds elephants, and lions, too."

Sohráb then asked, "There, on the right,

I see many horsemen, elephants, and gear,

A black pavilion stretching far, with ranks

I cannot count of soldiers on all sides.

Around it tents, behind it elephants,

In front are steeds of war. Before them waves

535 A banner figured with an elephant;

And golden-booted horsemen guard its gate."

"That's Tus, the son of Shah Nowzár," he said.

"That hero's emblem is the elephant."

دگر گفت کان سرخ پرده سرای

سواران بسی گردش اندر بپای

یکی شیر پیکر درفشی بزر

درفشان یکی در میانش گهر

چنین گفت کان فرّ آزادگان

جهانگیر گودرز کشوادگان

۵۴۰   بپرسید کان سبز پرده سرای

یکی لشکری گشن پیشش بپای

یکی تخت پرمایه اندر میان

زده پیش او اختر کاویان

ز هر کس که برپای پیشش براست

نشسته بیک رش سرش برتراست

یکی باره پیشش ببالای اوی

کمندی فرو هشته تا پای اوی

برو هر زمان بر خروشد همی

تو گویی که در زین بجوشد همی

۵۴۵   بسی پیل بر گستوان دار پیش

همی جوشد آن مرد بر جای خویش

نه مردست ز ایران ببالای اوی

نه بینم همی اسپ همتای اوی

درفشی بدید اژدها پیکرست

بران نیزه بر شیر زرّین سرست

چنین گفت کز چین یکی نامدار

He asked, "That red pavilion, whose is that?

There are mounted horsemen all around it, and on

Its banner there, a lion worked in gold

Whose center holds a single, shining jewel."

"That is Gudárz of Keshvád's camp," he said,

"The glory of Irán's nobility,"

540   He asked him then, "I see a green pavilion,

In front of which an army stands on guard.

A splendid throne is set there at its heart;

Before it stands the banner of Kavé.[23]

Who's seated there is taller by two hands

Than any noble standing by his side.

Before him there's a horse—a lasso hangs

Below its knees—that stands as tall as he.

From time to time he whinnies to his lord,

And stirs beneath his saddle like the sea.

545 Mailed elephants of war are near to hand,

And he himself sits restless in his place.

There's no one in Irán so tall as he,

Nor do I see a horse to equal his.

His standard's blazoned with a dragon's form,

And from its tip a golden lion roars."

He answered him, "He is a Chinese lord

بنوّی بیامد به شهریار

بپرسید نامش ز فرّخ هجیر

بدو گفت نامش ندارم بویر

۵۵۰ بدین دژ بدم من بدان روزگار

کجا او بیامد بر شهریار

غمی گشت سهراب را دل ازان

که جایی ز رستم نیامد نشان

نشان داده بود از پدر مادرش

همی دید و دیده نبد باورش

همی نام جست از زبان هجیر

مگر کان سخنها شود دلپذیر

نبشته بسر بر دگر گونه بود

ز فرمان نکاهد نخواهد فزود

۵۵۵ ازان پس بپرسید زان مهتران

کشیده سراپرده بد بر کران

سواران بسیار وپیلان پای

برآید همی نالهٔ کرّنای

یکی گرگ پیکر درفش از برش

برآورده از پرده زرّین سرش

بدو گفت کان پور گودرز گیو

که خوانند گردان ورا گیو نیو

ز گودرزیان مهتر وبهترست

به ایرانیان بر دوبهره سرست

Who's journeyed from his home to aid the shah."

"What is his name?" he asked the fortunate

Hojír. "I do not know his name," he answered him,

550 "For I was stationed at this fort when he

First came from China to the royal court."[24]

Sohráb despaired at heart. In all that camp,

No trace of Tahamtán had yet appeared.

His mother had described his father's signs.

He'd seen them all, but did not trust his eyes.

He pressed Hojír once more about Rostám,

And hoped his words would satisfy his heart,

His fate was written otherwise, alas,

And that command may not be changed by man.

555 He asked, "Who are the other nobles there,

Who've pitched their camp far on the army's flank,

With horsemen and with elephants drawn up?

I hear the sound of trumpets from their camp.

A banner with the figure of a wolf

Projects its tip above their golden tent."

"That's Giv, Gudárz's son," Hojír replied,

"He whom the other heroes call The Bold.

The eldest and the best of all his sons.

They think him twice a noble in Irán."[25]

۵۶۰ بدو گفت زان سوی تابنده شید
    برآید یکی پرده بینم سپید

ز دیبای رومی بپیشش سوار
    رده برکشیده فزون از هزار

پیاده سپردار و نیزه وران
    شده انجمن لشکری بی کران

نشسته سپهدار برتخت عاج
    نهاده بران عاج کرسی ساج

ز هودج فرو هشته دیبا جلیل
    غلام ایستاده رده خیل خیل

۵۶۵ بر خیمه نزدیک پرده سرای
    یکی ماه پیکر درفشی بپای

بدو گفت کورا فریبرز خوان
    که فرزند شاهست وتاج گوان

بپرسید کان سرخ پرده سرای
    بدهلیز چندی پیاده بپای

بگرد اندرش سرخ و زرد وبنفش
    ز هر گونهٔ برکشیده درفش

درفشی پس پشت پیکر گراز
    سرش ماه زرّین و بالا دراز

۵۷۰ چنین گفت کورا گرازست نام
    که در جنگ شیران ندارد لگام

هشیوار و ز تخمهٔ گیوگان
    که بر درد وسختی بندد میان

560   Sohráb then asked, "Beneath the morning sun

I see a white pavilion made of Greek

Brocade; before it stands a regiment

Of cavaliers more than a thousand strong.

A corps of infantry's assembled there

In endless ranks, all armed with shields and spears.

Their general's seated on an ivory throne,

On which they've placed a chair of polished teak.

Brocades of silk hang from his howdah's frame,

And rank on rank of slaves stand by his side.

565 Above a tent that's near this splendid camp,

A banner shows the figure of the moon."[26]

"He is the one whom we call Faribórz,

The son of Kay Kavús and heroes' crown."

      Sohráb asked him again, "That red pavilion,

Whose vestibule contains some guards on foot,

Around it banners yellow, red, and blue

Are spread upon the wind; behind them is

A lofty staff, tipped with a golden moon,

Whose standard bears the figure of a boar.

570 "His name," he said, "is Gorazé, who rides

Full tilt when lions are his prey. He's of

The clan of Giv, both vigilant and brave,

Undaunted by the pain and strain of war."

نشان پدر جست و با او نگفت

همی داشت آن راستی در نهفت

تو گیتی چه سازی که خود ساختست

جهاندار ازین کار پرداختست

زمانه نبشته دگر گونه داشت

چنان کو گذارد بباید گذاشت

۵۷۵   دگر باره پرسید ازان سرفراز

ازان کش بدیدار او بد نیاز

ازان پردهٔ سبز ومرد بلند

وزان اسپ و آن تاب داده کمند

از آن پس هجیر سپهبدش گفت

که از تو سخنرا چه باید نهفت

گر از نام چینی بمانم همی

ازان است کورا ندانم همی

بدو گفت سهراب کین نیست داد

ز رستم نکردی سخن هیچ یاد

۵۸۰   کسی کو بود پهلوان جهان

میان سپه در نماند نهان

تو گفتی که بر لشکر او مهترست

نگهبان هر مرز و هر کشورست

چنین داد پاسخ مر اورا هجیر

که شاید بدن کان گو شیر گیر

کنون رفته باشد بزابلستان

که هنگام بزمست در گلستان

بدو گفت سهراب کین خود مگوی

One sought his father's camp. One hid the truth,

And would not speak the words he longed to hear.

What can one do? This world's already made.

There is no task that He has left undone.

The writ of fate was otherwise, it seemed.

What it commands will finish as it must.

575   Once more he asked about that notable.

Once more he sought the one he longed to see:

That green pavilion and that giant man,

That massive horse, that twisted lariat.

Hojír the Turkish chief answered once more,

"Why should I hide the truth from you, great Prince?

If I withhold this Chinese prince's name,

The reason is that it's unknown to me."

"I'm sure this can't be true," Sohráb exclaimed.

When you have made no mention of Rostám.

580 The one who's *pahlaván* of all the world,

Could not be hidden here within this camp.

Did you not say he was the army's chief,

The one who keeps your border regions safe?"

Hojír responded to him in this way,

"That lion-slaying hero may perhaps

Have left the court to visit in Zaból.

It's spring, the time of wine and festival."

"Be still," Sohráb replied. "Don't waste such words

که دارد سپهد سوی جنگ روی

۵۸۵ برامش نشیند جهان پهلوان

برو بر بخندند پیر و جوان

مرا باتو امروز پیمان یکیست

بگوییم وگفتار ما اندکیست

اگر پهلوان را نمایی بمن

سرافراز باشی بهر انجمن

ترا بی نیازی دهم در جهان

گشاده کنم گنجهای نهان

ور ایدون که این راز داری ز من

گشاده بپوشی بمن بر سخن

۵۹۰ سرترا نخواهد همی تن بجای

نگر تا کدامین به آیدت رای

نبینی که موبد بخسرو چه گفت

بدانگه که بگشاد راز از نهفت

سخن گفت ناگفته چون گوهرست

کجا نابسوده بسنگ اندرست

چو از بند و پیوند یابد رها

درخشنده مهری بود بی بها

چنین داد پاسخ هجیرش که شاه

چو سیر آید از مهر وز تاج وگاه

۵۹۵ نبرد کسی جوید اندر جهان

که او ژنده پیل اندر آرد ز جان

کسیرا که رستم بود هم نبرد

On me. Kavús has marched into the field.

585 Were he to sit with minstrels now and drink,

Both young and old would laugh Rostám to shame.

The pact we've made today's a simple one.

I'll say it once, and in the fewest words.

If you identify Rostám to me,

You will be honored by your fellow men.

I'll open wide my treasury to you,

And give you wealth beyond your every need.

But if you hide this truth from me, and by

Your lying words conceal what is well known,

590 Your body will not keep its head for long.

Consider well. Which choice seems best to you?

A *mobad* gave his monarch this advice

When he'd revealed a secret of great worth,

'A word unspoken's like a gem,' he said,

'But rough, unpolished, trapped within the stone.

Yet once it's freed of fetters and of bonds,

It can become a shining, priceless jewel.' "

Hojír replied to him, "The shah, when he's

Grown weary of his crown and throne and seal,

595 Should seek to battle here that *pahlaván*

Who puts the elephant in fear of death.

Although his head should touch the sky, whoever

سرش ز آسمان اندر آید بگرد

تنش زور دارد بصد زورمند

سرش برترست از درخت بلند

چنو خشم گیرد بروز نبرد

چه هم رزم او ژنده پیل و چه مرد

بدو گفت سهراب از آزادگان

سیه بخت گودرز کشوادگان

۶۰۰   چرا چون ترا خواند باید پسر

بدین زور واین دانش واین هنر

تو مردان جنگی کجا دیدهٔ

که بانگ پی اسپ نشنیدهٔ

که چندین ز رستم سخن بایدت

زبان بر ستودنش بگشایدت

از آتش ترا بیم چندان بود

که دریا بآرام خندان بود

چو دریای سبز اندر آید ز جای

ندارد دم آتش تیز پای

۶۰۵   سر تیرگی اندر آید بخواب

چو تیغ از میان برکشد آفتاب

بدل گفت پس کاردیده هجیر

که گر من نشان گو شیر گیر

بگویم بدین ترک با زوردست

چنین یال و این خسروانی نشست

ز لشکر کند جنگ او و ز انجمن

Battles with Rostám will taste the earth.

His strength is greater than a hundred men's

His head outtops the tallest tree by far.

When he grows angry on the day of war,

No man or lion dares to face his wrath."

Sohráb replied, "Among the heroes of

Irán, Gudárz's fate is black as pitch!

600 When he's possessed of wisdom, strength, and skill,

Why must he call a wretch like you his son?

I doubt you've looked a warrior in the face,

Or even heard the sound of horses' hooves.

Yet now your speech is only of Rostám,

And every word you speak is lofty praise.

Perhaps, Hojír, you hold the fire in awe

Because the river's calm and smiling yet.

But when those emerald waters come to flood,

The hottest flame cannot withstand them long.

605 And when the sun draws forth its shining sword,

The night lays down its head in dark defeat."

The wise Hojír thought to himself, "Should I

Now show to him the lion-slayer's tent,

This fearsome Turk, who has such mighty arms,

And sits so royally upon his mount,

Will choose Rostám to fight from all this host,

برانگیزد این بارهٔ پیلتن

برین زور و این کتف و این یال اوی

شود کشته رستم بچنگال اوی

۶۱۰   از ایران نیاید کسی کینه خواه

بگیرد سر تخت کاؤس شاه

چنین گفت موبد که مردن بنام

به از زنده دشمن بدو شادکام

اگر من شوم کشته بردست اوی

نگردد سیه روز چون آب جوی

چو گودرز و هفتاد پور گزین

همه پهلوانان با آفرین

نباشد بایران تن من مباد

چنین دارم از موبد پاک یاد

۶۱۵   که چون برکشد از چمن بیخ سرو

سزد گر گیارا نبوید تذرو

بسهراب گفت این چه آشفتنست

همه با من از رستمت گفتنست

نباید ترا جست باو نبرد

برآرد به آوردگاه از تو گرد

همی پیلتن را نخواهی شکست

همانا که آسان نیاید بدست

چون بشنید این گفتهای درشت

نهان کرد ازو روی و بنمود پشت

When he spurs his massive steed into the field.

And with his strength, his neck, and chest, I fear

Rostám will perish in his grip. In all

610 Irán what man is there who'll seek revenge?

Sohráb will seize the throne of Shah Kavús.

The *mobad*s say that death with honor's better

Than a life that's pleasing to one's foes.

If he should slay me now, the day will not

Turn black, nor will the rivers run with blood.

If Gudarz and his seventy heroic sons,

All worthy *pahlaváns*, should vanish from

Irán, then may I also cease to be.

I've heard the *mobad*s say that once the cypress

615 Tree's uprooted from the plain, the scent

Of other plants won't keep the pheasants there."

Hojír replied, "Why are you angry now?

It's you whose speech is only of Rostám.

Don't fight with him, or on the battlefield

He'll swiftly stretch you in the dust.

You won't defeat Rostám, don't even try.

Nor can you hope to capture him with ease."

§ *The Challenge*

When he had heard these words, Sohráb first turned

His back to him and hid his face, then spun

۶۲۰   ز بالا زدش تند یک پشتِ دست

بیفگند و آمد بجای نشست

بپوشید خفتان و برسرنهاد

یکی خود چینی بکردار باد

ز تندی بجوش آمدش خون برگ

نشست از بر بارهٔ تیزتنگ

خروشید و بگرفت نیزه بدست

به آوردگه رفت چون پیل مست

کس از نامداران ایران سپاه

نیارست کردن بدو در نگاه

۶۲۵   ز پای و رکیب و ز دست و عنان

ز بازوی و ز آب داده سنان

ازان پس دلیران شدند انجمن

بگفتند کاینت گو پیلتن

نشاید نگه کردن آسان بدوی

که یارد شدن پیش او جنگجوی

ازان پس خروشید سهراب گرد

همی شاه کاوس را بر شمرد

چنین گفت با شاه آزاد مرد

که چون است کارت بدشت نبرد

۶۳۰   چرا کردهٔ نام کاؤس کی

که در جنگ نه تاو داری نه پی

تنت را برین نیزه بریان کنم

620   Around and struck Hojír a fearful blow

That felled him there. And then he sought his tent.

There like the wind, he donned his coat of mail

And on his head he placed his Chinese casque.

His rage had made the blood boil in his veins.

He seized his lance, mounted his swift-paced horse,

Then roaring in his fury like a maddened

Elephant, he rushed onto the field.

There was no famous hero of Irán

Who even dared to look upon Sohráb—

625   That sturdy leg and thigh, that hand and rein,

Those mighty arms and finely polished lance.

The stalwarts of Irán assembled there

Exclaimed, "this surely is the *pahlaván* Rostám;

One almost fears to look on him.

Who here will dare to challenge him to fight?"

Sohráb the hero roared his defiance,

And poured his curses on Kavús the shah.

The noble Sohráb addressed him tauntingly,

"What busines do you have upon this field,

630   Why do you call yourself Kavús the shah,

When in a fight you've neither strength nor pluck?

I'll spit your body on this lance,

ستاره بدین کار گریان کنم

یکی سخت سوگند خوردم ببزم

بدان شب کجا کشته شد ژند رزم

کز ایران نمانم یکی نیزه دار

کنم زنده کاؤس کی را بدار

که داری از ایرانیان. تیزچنگ

که پیش من آید بهنگام جنگ

۶۳۵   همی گفت و می بود جوشان بسی

از ایران ندادند پاسخ کسی

خروشان بیامد بپرده سرای

بنیزه در آورد بالا ز جای

خم آورد زان پس سنان کرد سیخ

بزد نیزه برکند هفتاد میخ

سراپرده یک بهره آمد ز پای

ز هر سو برآمد دم گَرْتای

رمید آن دلاور سپاه دلیر

بکردار گوران ز چنگال شیر

۶۴۰   غمی گشت کاؤس و آواز داد

کزین نامداران فرّخ نژاد

یکی نزد رستم برید آگهی

کزین ترک شد مغز گردان تهی

ندارم سواری ورا هم نبرد

از ایران نیارد کس این کار کرد

بشد طوس و پیغام کاوس برد

شنیده سخن پیش او بر شمرد

And set the stars to weeping with one blow.

The night they slew brave Zhende Razm, I swore

A solemn oath to seek revenge in war.

Here in Irán I'll spare no one who bears

A lance, and Shah Kavús I'll crucify.

Of all Irán's swift-handed *pahlaváns*,

Do you have one to face me here and fight?"

635 Sohráb spoke thus, his words boiled up with rage,

But from Irán none rose to answer him.

He roared aloud and set upon their camp;

He scattered tethered horses with his lance's butt,

Then bending low, he used its sharpened tip

To pluck some seventy pegs out of the earth.

The palace tent came crashing down at once,

And from all sides the buglers blew retreat.

The army of Irán fled from Sohráb

Like onagers who flee the lion's claws.

640 In his distress Kavús cried out,

"Choose one among the well-born notables

And send him to Rostám with news of this.

Tell him that fear has struck our heroes dumb.

I've not one horseman who's the equal of

This dreadful Turk, not one to challenge him."

Tus rushed to tell Rostám the shah's command,

Repeating for him what Kavús had said.

بدو گفت رستم که هر شهریار

که کردی مرا ناگهان خواستار

۶۴۵   گهی جنگ بودی گهی ساز بزم

ندیدم ز کاؤس جز رنج رزم

بفرمود تا رخش را زین کنند

سواران بروها پر از چین کنند

ز خیمه نگه کرد رستم بدشت

زره گیو را دید کاندر گذشت

نهاد از بر رخش رخشنده زین

همی گفت گرگین که بشتاب هین

همی بست بر باره رهام تنگ

ببر گستوان بر زده طوس چنگ

۶۵۰   همی این بدان آن بدین گفت زود

تهمتن چو از خیمه آوا شنود

بدل گفت کین کار آهرمنست

نه این رستخیز از پی یکتنست

بزد دست وپوشید ببر بیان

ببست آن کیانی کمر برمیان

نشست از بر ِ رخش وبگرفت راه

زواره نگهبان ِ گاه وسپاه

درفشش ببردند بااو بهم

همی رفت پرخاشجوی و دژم

۶۵۵   چو سهراب را دید با یال وشاخ

برش چون بر ِ سام جنگی فراخ

Rostám replied, "The other shahs who've called

On me when they'd some pressing need, sometimes

645   Invited me to battle, sometimes to feast.

Kavús has shown me but the pain of war."

He ordered that they saddle Rakhsh and that

His horsemen now set frowns upon their brows.

From his tent, Rostám looked on the field and saw

That noble Giv was galloping toward

The battlefield. He put his saddle on

The shining Rakhsh. Gorgín urged him to haste.

Rohám made tight the cinch while noble Tus

Was swiftly buckling on its coat of mail,

650   Each one urging the other to be quick.

Within his tent, Rostám could hear the din.

"This is the work of Ahrimán," he thought,[27]

This turmoil's not the work of just one man."

He quickly seized his tiger-skin cuirass,

And tied the royal belt around his waist,

Then mounted Rakhsh and rode to war. He left

His brother, Zavaré, to guard the army.

They bore his banner at his side, and as

He rode along, rage mounted in his heart.

655   When he could see Sohráb, his neck and arms,

His chest as broad as that of warlike Sam,

بدو گفت از ایدر بیکسو شویم

بآوردگه هر دو همرو شویم

بمالید سهراب کف را بکف

باوردگه رفت از پیش صف

برستم چنین گفت کاندر گذشت

ز من جنگ و پیگار سوی تو گشت

از ایران نخواهی دگر یار کس

چو من باتو باشم بآورد بس

۶۶۰   به آوردگه بر ترا جای نیست

ترا خود بیک مشت من پای نیست

ببالا بلندی و با کتف و یال

ستم یافت بالت ز بسیار سال

نگه کرد رستم بدان سرفراز

بدان چنگ و یال و رکیب دراز

بدو گفت نرم ای جوان مرد گرم

زمین سرد وخشک وسخن گرم ونرم

بپیری بسی دیدم آوردگاه

بسی بر زمین پست کردم سپاه

۶۶۵   تبه شد بسی دیو در جنگ من

ندیدم بدان سو که بودم شکن

نگه کن مرا گر ببینی بجنگ

اگر زنده مانی مترس از نهنگ

مرا دید در جنگ دریا وکوه

He called to him "Let's move a little way

Apart, and face each other on the field."

Sohráb just rubbed his hands together and

Moved off to wait before the battle lines.

He told Rostám, "I've shown my readiness

For war. It's you who now must choose to fight.

Don't look to any in Irán for help.

It is enough when you and I are here.

660 You don't belong upon the battlefield.

You can't withstand a single blow of mine.

Although you're tall in stature and you have

A mighty chest, your wings now droop with age."

Rostám looked on that noble face, that fist

And neck, that massive leg, and said with warmth,

"Oh, savage youth. Your speech is full of heat.

Alas, the earth is dry and cold. In my

Long years I've looked on many battlefields,

And I've stretched many foes upon the ground.

665 Not few the demons I've slain with my two hands,

And nowhere have I ever known defeat.

Look on me now. When you have fought with me,

And lived, you need not fear the crocodile.

The mountains and the sea know what I've done

که با نامداران توران گروه

چه کردم ستاره گوای منست

بمردی جهان زیر پای منست

بدو گفت کز تو بپرسم سخن

همه راستی باید افگند بن

۶۷۰   من ایدون گمانم که تو رستمی

گر از تخمهٔ نامور نیرمی

چنین داد پاسخ که رستم نیم

هم از تخمهٔ سامِ نیرم نیم

که او پهلوانست و من کهترم

نه با تخت وگاهم نه با افسرم

از امید سهراب شد ناامید

برو تیره شد روی روز سپید

به آوردگه رفت نیزه بکفت

همی ماند از گفت مادر شگفت

۶۷۵   یکی تنگ میدان فرو ساختند

بکوتاه نیزه همی تاختند

نماند ایچ بر نیزه بند وسنان

بچپ باز بردند هر دو عنان

بشمشیر هندی برآویختند

همی ز آهن آتش فرو ریختند

بزخم اندرون تیغ شد ریز ریز

To all the bravest heroes of Turán.

The stars bear witness too. In manliness

And bravery the world is at my feet.

Sohráb replied, "I have a single question,

But you must answer it with truth. I think

670 That you must be Rostám, or that you are

The seed of Narimán. Is this not so?"

Rostám replied to him, "I am not he,

Nor descended from great Sam or Narimán.

Rostám's a *pahlaván*, I'm less than he.

I have no throne, no palace, and no crown."

From hope Sohráb was cast into despair.

The day's bright face now turned to darkest night.

§ *The First Battle*

He rode onto the battlefield, armed with

His lance and wondering at his mother's words.

675 Upon the field of war they chose a narrow

Space to meet and fought with shortened lance.

When neither points nor bindings held,

They reined their horses in and turned aside,

And then with Indian swords renewed their fight.

Sparks pouring from their iron blades like rain.

With blows they shattered both their polished swords.

چه زخمی که پیدا کند رستخیز

گرفتند زان پس عمود گران

غمی گشت بازوی کند آوران

۶۸۰   ز نیرو عمود اندر آورد خم

دمان باد پایان و گردان دژم

ز اسپان فرو ریخت بر گستوان

زره پاره شد بر میان گوان

فرو ماند اسپ و دلاور ز کار

یکی را نبد چنگ و بازو بکار

تن از خوی پرآب و همه کام خاک

زبان گشته از تشنگی چاک چاک

یک از یگدگر ایستادند دور

پر از درد باب و پر از رنج پور

۶۸۵   جهانا شکفتی ز کردار تست

هم از تو شکسته هم از تو درست

ازین دو یکی را نجنبید مهر

خرد دور بد مهر ننمود چهر

همی بچّه را باز داند ستور

چه ماهی بدریا چه در دشت گور

نداند همی مردم از رنج و آز

یکی دشمنی را ز فرزند باز

همی گفت رستم که هرگز نهنگ

ندیدم که آید بدین سان بجنگ

۶۹۰   مرا خوار شد جنگ دیو سپید

Such blows as these will fall on Judgment Day.

And then each hero seized his heavy mace.

The battle had now wearied both their arms.

680   Although their mounts were neighing and both heroes

Groaned with pain, they bent them with their might.

The armor flew from their two steeds; the links

That held their coats of mail burst wide apart.

Both mounts stood still; nor could their masters move.

Not one could lift a hand or arm to fight.

Their bodies ran with sweat, dirt filled their mouths,

And heat and thirst had split their tongues. Once more

They faced each other on that plain—the son

Exhausted and the father weak with pain.

685   Oh, world! How strange your workings are! From you

Comes both what's broken and what's whole as well.

Of these two men, neither was stirred by love.

Wisdom was far off, the face of love not seen.

From fishes in the sea to wild horses on

The plain, all beasts can recognize their young.

But man who's blinded by his wretched pride,

Cannot distinguish son from foe.

    Rostám said to himself, "I've never seen

A warlike crocodile that fought like this.

690   My battle with the Div Sepíd seems nothing now.[28]

ز مردی شد امروز دل ناامید

جوانی چنین ناسپرده جهان

نه گردی نه نام آوری از مهان

بسیری رسانیدم از روزگار

دو لشکر نظاره بدین کارزار

چو آسوده شد بارهٔ هر دو مرد

ز آورد و ز بند و ننگ و نبرد

بزه بر نهادند هر دو کمان

جوانه همان سالخورده همان

۶۹۵   زره بود و خفتان و ببر بیان

ز کلک و ز پیکانش نامد زیان

غمی شد دل هر دو از یکدگر

گرفتند هر دو دوال کمر

تهمتن که گر دست بردی بسنگ

بکندی ز کوه سیه روز جنگ

کمر بند سهراب را چاره کرد

که بر زین بجنباند اندر نبرد

میان جوان را نبود آگهی

بماند از هنر دست رستم تهی

۷۰۰   دو شیر اوژن از جنگ سیر آمدند

همه خسته وگشته دیر آمدند

دگر باره سهراب گرز گران

ز زین برکشید وبیفشارد ران

بزد گرز و آورد کتفش بدرد

Today my heart despaired of my own strength

While these two armies watched us here,

A youth who's seen but little of the world,

And who is neither noble nor well known,

Has made me weary of my destiny."

When both their steeds had rested and they had

Recovered from the pain and shame of war,

These mighty warriors, one ancient and

The other still a youth, both strung their bows.

695 But since each wore a breast plate and a tiger-

Skin cuirass, their arrows could not penetrate.

Although each now despaired before his foe,

They closed and seized each other round the waist.

Rostám, who in the heat of battle, could wrench

Huge stones from the flinty earth with his bare hands,

Now grasped Sohráb around the waist,

And sought with all his strength to wrest him from

His horse's back. The youth budged not at all.

The hero's mighty grip left him unmoved.

700 These lion-slayers both grew weary then.

They paused to rest and ease their wounds awhile.

And then once more Sohráb drew out his mace,

And pressed his thighs into his horse's flanks.

He struck Rostám upon the shoulder once,

بپیچید و درد از دلیری بخورد

بخندید سهراب وگفت ای سوار

بزخم دلیران نۀ پایدار

برزم اندرون رخش گویی خرست

دودست سوار از همه بترست

۷۰۵   اگر چه گوی سرو بالا بود

جوانی کند پیر کانا بود

بسستی رسید این ازان آن ازین

چنان تنگ شد بر دلیران زمین

که از یکدگر روی برگاشتند

دل و جان باندوه بگذاشتند

تهمتن بتوران سپه شد بجنگ

بدانسان که نخچیر بیند پلنگ

میان سپاه اندر آمد چو گرگ

پراگنده گشت آن سپاه بزرگ

۷۱۰   عنان را به پیچید سهراب گرد

بایرانیان بر یکی حمله برد

بزد خویشتن را بایران سپاه

ز گرزش بسی نامور شد تباه

دل رستم اندیشۀ کرد بد

که کاؤس را بی گمان بد رسد

ازین پرهنر ترک نو خاسته

بخفتان بر و بازو آراسته

بلشکرگه خویش تازید زود

A fearful blow that made him wince with pain.

Sohráb just laughed at him, "Oh, *pahlaván*!

It seems you cannot bear a warrior's blow.

This steed of yours in battle is an ass.

Or is it that his master's hands grow weak?

705 Although you're tall as any cypress tree,

An old man who would play the youth's a fool."

But each was wearied by the other now.

The earth seemed strait to them, the end unsure.

They turned their steeds aside and left the field,

Abandoning their hearts and souls to grief.

Great Tahamtán attacked the Turkish host

Just like a leopard when he spies his prey.

When that fierce wolf appeared within their ranks,

The army of Turán all turned and fled.

710 Sohráb had turned his horse toward Irán,

And fell upon their camp in swift assault.

He launched himself into their very midst,

Slaughtering many heroes with his mace.

Rostám grew anxious when he learned of this.

He thought that he would surely harm Kavús—

This wondrous Turk who had so suddenly

Appeared with chest and arms adorned for war.

He galloped swiftly to his army's camp,

که اندیشهٔ دل بدان گونه بود

۷۱۵   میان سپه دید سهراب را

چو می لعل کرده بخون آب را

سرنیزه پر خون و خفتان و دست

تو گفتی ز نخچیر گشتست مست

غمی گشت رستم چو اورا بدید

خروشی چو شیر ژیان برکشید

بدو گفت کای ترک خونخواره مرد

از ایران سپه جنگ باتو که کرد

چرا دست یازی بسوی همه

چو گرگ آمدی در میان رمه

۷۲۰   بدو گفت سهراب توران سپاه

ازین رزم بودند بر بی گناه

تو آهنگ کردی بدیشان نخست

کسی باتو پیکار وکینه نجست

بدو گفت رستم که شد تیره روز

چه پیدا کند تیغ گیتی فروز

برین دشت هم دار و هم منبرست

که روشن جهان زیر تیغ اندرست

گر ایدون که شمشیر با بوی شیر

چنین آشنا شد تو هرگز ممیر

۷۲۵   بگردیم شبگیر باتیغ کین

برو تاچه خواهد جهان آفرین

So greatly was Rostám distressed by this.

715   Within the army's heart he saw Sohráb.

He'd turned the river there wine red with blood.

His spear was drenched in gore, his breast and arms

As well. He seemed a hunter drunk with sport.

Rostám grew sick at heart as he looked on,

And roared in anger like a fearsome lion.

"You cruel bloodthirsty Turk! Which of the men

Assembled here has challenged you to fight?

Why did you raise your hand in war to them?

Why slaughter them, a wolf among the flock?"

720   Sohráb replied, "The army of Turán

Was blameless in this fight as well. You first

Attacked, though none was keen to challenge you."

"The day's grown dark," Rostám replied, "but when

Once more the world-illuming sun's bright blade

Appears, there'll be a gibbet and a throne.

Set side by side upon this plain of war.

The whole bright world now lies beneath the sword.

Although your blade's familiar with the smell

Of milk, may you live long and never die.

725   Let us return at dawn with our keen swords.

Go now; await the World Creator's wish."

برفتند و روی هوا تیره گشت

ز سهراب گردون همی خیره گشت

تو گفتی ز جنگش سرشت آسمان

نیارامد از تاختن یک زمان

وگر باره زیر اندرش آهنست

شگفتی روانست و رویین تنست

شب تیره آمد سوی لشکرش

میان سوده از جنگ و از خنجرش

۷۳۰ بهومان چنین گفت کامروز هور

برآمد جهان کرد پر جنگ وشور

شما را چه کرد آن سوار دلیر

که یال یلان داشت و آهنگ شیر

بدو گفت هومان که فرمان شاه

چنان بد کز ایدر نجنبد سپاه

همه کار ما سخت ناساز بود

باورد گشتن چه آغاز بود

بیامد یکی مرد پرخاشجوی

برین لشکر گشن بنهاد روی

۷۳۵ تو گفتی ز مستی کنون خاستست

وگر جنگ با یکتن آراستست

چنین گفت سهراب کو زین سپاه

نکرد از دلیران کسیرا تباه

از ایرانیان من بسی کشته ام

§ *The Interval*

They left and then the sky turned black. The circling

Sphere looked down and wondered at Sohráb.

It seemed that he'd been formed for war and strife.

He rested not a moment from attack.

The steed he rode was made of steel, his soul

A wonder, and his body hardened brass.

Sohráb came to his camp when night had fallen,

His body scoured with wounds. He asked Humán,

730 "Today the rising sun filled all the world

With weapons and the sounds of war. Tell me,

What damage did he wreak upon our host,

That horseman with a hero's neck and lion's charge?"

Humán replied, "The shah's command to me

Was that the army should not stir from here.

We were quite unprepared. We had not looked

To fight at all today. When suddenly

A fierce and warlike man approached our camp,

And turned to face this broad-ranged company,

735 It seemed he'd just returned from drinking or

From battling singlehanded with some foe."

Sohráb replied, "And yet he did not slay

A single man from all this numerous host,

While I slew many heroes from Irán,

زمین را بخون وگل آغشته ام

کنون خوان همی باید آراستن

بباید بمی غم ز دل کاستن

وزان روی رستم سپه را بدید

سخن راند با گیو وگفت و شنید

۷۴۰   که امروز سهراب رزم آزمای

چگونه بجنگ اندر آورد پای

چنین گفت با رستم گُرد گیو

کزین گونه هرگز ندیدیم نیو

بیامد دمان تا بقلب سپاه

ز لشکر بر طوس شد کینه خواه

که او بود برزین و نیزه بدست

چو گرگین فرود آمد او برنشست

بیامد چو بانیزه او را بدید

بکردار شیر ژیان بردمید

۷۴۵   عمودی خمیده بزد بر برش

زنیرو بیفتاد ترگ از سرش

نتابید با او بتابید روی

شدند از دلیران بسی جنگ جوی

ز گردان کسی مایهٔ او نداشت

جز از پیلتن پایهٔ او نداشت

هم آیین پیشین نگه داشتیم

سپاهی برو ساده بگماشتیم

سواری نشد پیش او یکتنه

And made that campground muddy with their blood.

But now it's time to spread the board and feast.

Come, let's ease our hearts with ruby wine."

While on the other side, Rostám reviewed

His troops and spoke a while with Giv. "How did

740   The battle-tried Sohráb fare here today?"

Did he attack the camp? How did he fight?"

Heroic Giv replied to Tahamtán,

"I've never seen a hero quite like him.

He galloped to the army's very heart.

And there within that host made straight for Tus,

For he was armed and mounted, lance in hand.

And while Gorgín dismounted, he sat firm.

He came and when he saw him with his lance,

He galloped toward him like a raging lion.

745   He bent his heavy mace upon his chest.

Its force unloosed his helmet from his head.

Tus saw that he must fail, and turned and fled.

Then many other warriors challenged him,

But none among those heroes had his strength.

Only Piltán's the equal of this youth.

And yet we still held fast our ancient rule,

And held the army in a single rank.

No horseman went to fight with him alone.

همی تاخت از قلب تا میمنه

۷۵۰   غمی گشت رستم ز گفتار اوی

بر شاه کاؤس بنهاد روی

چو کاؤس کی پهلوان را بدید

بر خویش نزدیک جایش گزید

ز سهراب رستم زبان بر گشاد

ز بالا و برزش همی کرد یاد

که کس در جهان کودک نارسید

بدین شیر مردی و گردی ندید

ببالا ستاره بساید همی

تنش را زمین بر گراید همی

۷۵۵   دو بازو و رانش ز ران هیون

همانا که دارد ستبری فزون

بگرز و بتیغ و بتیر وکمند

ز هر گونهٔ آزمودیم بند

سرانجام گفتم که من پیش ازین

بسی گرد را بر گرفتم ز زین

گرفتم دوال کمربند اوی

بیفشاردم سخت پیوند اوی

همی خواستم کش ز زین برکنم

چو دیگر کسانش بخاک افگنم

۷۶۰   گر از باد جنبان شود کوه خار

نجنبید بر زین بر آن نامدار

چو فردا بیاید بدشت نبرد

While he paraded on the field of war."

750 Rostám was grieved at this report. He turned

His face toward the camp of Shah Kavús.

When Kay Kavús saw him entering his tent,

He sat the *pahlaván* close by his throne.

Rostám described Sohráb to him, and spoke

At length of his great stature and his strength.

"None in this world has ever seen a child

Half grown who is so brave, so lionlike.

His head brushes against the stars above,

The earth below bends at his body's weight.

755 His arms and thighs are like a camel's limbs,

And yet to me they seemed more massive still.

We fought at length with heavy mace and sword,

With bow and arrow, and with lasso too.

No feint or weapon did we leave untried.

And finally I said, 'Before this time

I've lifted many heroes from their seats,'

And seized him round the waist and grasped his belt.

I thought to pluck him from his horse's back

And hurl him like the others to the ground.

760 The hurricane that shakes a granite peak

Would not disturb that worthy in his seat.

Tomorrow when he rides into the field,

بکشتی همی بایدم چاره کرد

بکوشم ندانم که پیروز کیست

ببینیم تا رای یزدان به چیست

کزویست پیروزی و فرّ و زور

هم او آفرینندهٔ ماه و هور

بدو گفت کاؤس یزدان پاک

دل بدسگالت کند چاک چاک

۷۶۵   من امشب بپیش جهان آفرین

بمالم فراوان دو رخ بر زمین

کزویست پیروزی و دستگاه

بفرمان او تابد از چرخ ماه

کند تازه این بار کام ترا

برآرد بخورشید نام ترا

بدو گفت رستم که با فرّ شاه

برآید همه کامهٔ نیک خواه

بلشکرگه خویش بنهاد روی

پر اندیشه جان و سرش کینه جوی

۷۷۰   زواره بیامد خَلیده روان

که چون بود امروز بر پهلوان

ازو خوردنی خواست رستم نخست

پس آنگه ز اندیشهگان دل بشست

چنین راند پیش برادر سخن

که بیدار دل باش و تندی مکن

بشبگیر چون من بآوردگاه

My only hope's to fight him hand to hand.

And though I'll strive, I don't know who will win.

Nor do I know what choice Yazdán will make.

Strength, victory, and fame all come from Him

Who has created both the sun and moon."

Kavús replied, "Then may the Pure Lord split

In two the hearts of all who wish you ill!

765　Tonight before the Maker of the World

I'll press my brow and cheeks against the earth.

For strength and greatness come from Him alone.

By his command the moon sends down its light.

Once more may He renew your hopes, and raise

Your name aloft in triumph to the sun."

Rostám replied, "By the glory of the shah,

May the hopes of those who wish him well be heard."

　　Brave Tahamtán returned to camp, his soul

Distressed, his mind prepared for war.

770　His brother, Zavaré, approached him with

An anxious heart. "How did you fare today?"

Rostám first called for food, and ate his fill,

Then purged his heart of all his grief and fear.

He spoke to Zavaré, advising him,

"Be vigilant of heart, do nothing rash.

Tomorrow, just at dawn, when I must meet

روم پیش آن ترک آوردخواه

بیاور سپاه و درفش مرا

همان تخت و زرّینه کفش مرا

۷۷۵   همی باش بر پیش پرده سرای

چو خورشید تابان برآید ز جای

گر ایدون که پیروز باشم بجنگ

به آوردگه بر نسازم درنگ

وگر خود دگر گونه گردد سخن

تو زاری میاغاز و تندی مکن

مباشید یکتن برین رزمگاه

مسازید جستن سوی رزم راه

یکایک سوی زابلستان شوید

از ایدر بنزدیک دستان شوید

۷۸۰   تو خرسند گردان دل مادرم

چنین کرد یزدان قضا برسرم

بگویش که تو دل بمن در مبند

که سودی نداردت بودن نژند

کس اندر جهان جاودانه نماند

ز گردون مرا خود بهانه نماند

بسی شیر و دیو و پلنگ و نهنگ

تبه شده بچنگم بهنگام جنگ

بسی باره و دژ که کردیم پست

نیاورد کس دست من زیردست

۷۸۵   درمرگ را آن بکوبد که پای

That warlike Turk in battle once again,

You bring the army and my standard to

The field, my throne and golden boots as well.

775 Be standing at the door of my pavilion

When the shining sun begins to rise.

If in this fight I gain the victory,

I will not linger on the battlefield.

But should the matter turn out otherwise,

Don't weep for me, and do not seek revenge.

Neither enter the field to fight alone,

Nor yet prepare yourself for general war.

Return together to Zabolestán,

Once you are there, seek out my father, Zal.

780 Then you must try to ease my mother's heart.

This is the fate Yazdán decreed for me.

Tell her she should not mourn for me too long,

For she will do herself no good by that.

No one has lived for all eternity.

I've no complaint against the circling sphere.

In battle have I strangled many demons,

And lions, crocodiles, and leopards too.

I've leveled forts and towers to the ground,

And there's no man who's ever vanquished me.

785 The man who mounts a horse and gallops off

باسپ اندر آرد بجنبد ز جای

اگر سال گشتی فزون از هزار

همین بود خواهد سرانجام کار

چو خرسند گردد بدستان بگوی

که از شاه گیتی مبرتاب روی

اگر جنگ سازد تو سستی مکن

چنان رو که او راند از بن سخن

همه مرگ راییم پیر و جوان

بگیتی نماند کسی جاودان

۷۹۰   ز شب نیمهٔ گفتِ سهراب بود

دگر نیمه آرامش و خواب بود

وزان روی سهراب با انجمن

همی می گساريد با رودزن

بهومان چنین گفت کین شیر مرد

که بامن همی گردد اندر نبرد

ز بالای من نیست بالاش کم

برزم اندرون دل ندارد دژم

برو کتف و یالش همانند من

تو گوئی که داننده بر زد رَسَن

۷۹۵   نشانهای مادر بیابم همی

بدان نیز لختی بتابم همی

گمانی برم من که او رستمست

که چون او بگیتی نبرده کمست

نباید که من باپدر جنگ جوی

To fight, is he not knocking on death's door?

And if you live a thousand years, or more,

At last, the end of all will be the same.

When she's content, then tell Dastán, 'Don't turn

Your back upon the monarch of the world.

Should he make war, do not be slack in your

Support, obey his word in everything.

We all are mortal, young and old alike.

There's none who lives for all eternity.'"

790 For half that night their words were of Sohráb.

The other half they spent in restful sleep.

     In the Turkish camp, Sohráb with all his friends

Had passed the night with wine and minstrelsy.

Musing, to Humán he said, "This lion who

Engages me so fiercely on the field,

Is not one whit less tall than I, and when

Engaged in single combat has no fear.

His shoulders, chest, and neck are so like mine,

It seems some craftsman marked them with a rule.

795 I see in him the signs my mother told

Me of. That makes me hesitate a little.

I think that he must be Rostám, for in

This world few *pahlaváns* can equal him.

I must not in confusion rush to meet

شوم خیره روی اندر آرم بروی

بدو گفت هومان که در کارزار

رسیدست رستم بمن اند بار

شنیدم که درجنگ مازندران

چه کرد آن دلاور بگرز گران

۸۰۰   بدین رخش ماند همی رخش اوی

ولیکن ندارد پی و پخش اوی

چو خورشید تابان برآورد پر

سیه زاغ پرّان فرو برد سر

تهمتن بپوشید بَبر بیان

نشست از بر ژنده پیل ژیان

کمندی بفتراک بربست شست

یکی تیغ هندی گرفته بدست

بیامد بران دشت آوردگاه

نهاده بسر بر ز آهن کلاه

۸۰۵   همه تلخی از بهر بیشی بود

مبادا که با آز خویشی بود

بپوشید سهراب خفتان رزم

سرش پر ز رزم و دلش پر ز بزم

بیامد خروشان بران دشت جنگ

بچنگ اندرون گرزهٔ گاو رنگ

ز رستم بپرسید خندان دولب

My father here in combat face to face."

Humán replied, "I've met Rostám in war,

And seen him battle many times. I've heard

How that brave hero used his heavy mace

When he was fighting in Mazandarán.

800 This horse of his is very like Rostám's,

But he has not the hoof or rump of Rakhsh."

§ *The Second Day*

The shining sun spread wide its radiance,

The raven tucked its head beneath its wings,

Tahmatán put on his tiger-skin cuirass,

And sat astride his huge, fierce elephant.

To his seat he bound his rope in sixty coils,

And in his hand he grasped an Indian sword.

He galloped to the field, the place where they

Would fight, and there put on his iron helm.

805 All bitterness is born of precedence.

Alas when it is yoked to greedy pride!

Sohráb stood up and armed himself. His head

Was filled with war, his heart with revelry.

Shouting his cry he rode into the field,

Within his hand, he held his bullhide mace.

He greeted him, a smile upon his lips,

تو گفتی که با او بهم بود شب

که شب چون بُدت روز چون خاستی

ز پیگار بر دل چه آراستی

۸۱۰ ز کف بفگن این گرز و شمشیر کین

بزن جنگ و بیداد را برزمین

نشینیم هر دو پیاده بهم

بمی تازه داریم روی دژم

بپیش جهاندار پیمان کنیم

دل از جنگ جستن پشیمان کنیم

همان تا کسی دیگر آید برزم

تو با من بساز و بیارای بزم

دل من همی با تو مهر آورد

همی آب شرمم بچهر آورد

۸۱۵ همانا که داری ز گردان نژاد

کنی پیش من گوهر خویش یاد

مگر پوردستان سام یلی

گزین نامور رستم زابلی

بدو گفت رستم که ای نامجوی

نبودیم هرگز بدین گفت و گوی

ز کشتی گرفتن سخن بود دوش

نگیرم فریب تو زین در مکوش

نه من کودکم گر تو هستی جوان

بکشتی کمر بسته ام بر میان

۸۲۰ بکوشیم و فرجام کار آن بود

As though they'd spent the night in company.

"How did you sleep? How do you feel today?

And how have you prepared yourself to fight?

810 Let's put aside this mace and sword of war.

Cast strife and wrong down to the ground.

Let us dismount and sit together now,

And smooth our brows with wine. And let us make

A pact before the World Preserving Lord,

That we'll repent of all our warlike plans.

Until another comes who's keen to fight,

Make peace with me and let us celebrate.

My heart is ever moved by love for you,

And wets my face with tears of modesty.

815 I'm sure you're from a noble line, come then,

Recite for me the line of your descent.

Aren't you the son of brave Dastán, the son

Of Sam? Aren't you the *pahlaván* Rostám?"[29]

"Oh, shrewd ambitious youth," Rostám replied,

"Before this hour we never spoke like this.

Last night our words were of the coming fray.

Your tricks won't work with me; don't try again.

Though you are but a youth, I am no child,

And I'm prepared to fight you hand to hand.

820 So let's begin our strife. Its end will be

که فرمان ورای جهان بان بود

بسی گشته ام در فراز و نشیب

نیم مرد گفتار و بند و فریب

بدو گفت سهراب کز مرد پیر

نباشد سخن زین نشان دلبذیر

مرا آرزو بد که در بسترت

برآید بهنگام هوش از برت

کسی کز تو ماند ستودان کند

بپرّد روان تن بزندان کند

۸۲۵　اگر هوش تو زیر دست منست

بفرمان یزدان بساییم دست

از اسپان جنگی فرود آمدند

هشیوار با گبر و خود آمدند

ببستند بر سنگ اسپ نبرد

برفتند هر دو روان پر ز گرد

بکشتی گرفتن برآویختند

ز تن خون و خوی را فرو ریختند

بزد دست سهراب چون پیل مست

بر آوردش از جای و بنهاد پست

۸۳۰　بکردار شیری که برگور نر

زند چنگ و گور اندر آید بسر

نشست از بر سینهٔ پیل تن

پر از خاک چنگال و روی و دهن

یکی خنجری آبگون بر کشید

As the Keeper of the World commands it should.

I've traveled long through hills and valleys too.

And I'm no man for guile, deceits, and lies."

Sohráb replied, "Such words do not befit

A warrior who's so advanced in years.

I wished that you might die upon your bed,

And that your soul would leave in its own time;

That those you leave behind could keep your bones,

Immure your flesh, but let your spirit fly.[30]

825   But if your life is in my grasp, then as

Yazdán commands, let us lock hands and fight."

They both dismounted from their horses and

In helmet and mail they approached each other

with care. They tied their horses to a stone.

Then advanced on foot, their hearts as cold as earth.

Each seized the other and they grappled until

Their bodies ran with sweat and blood. Sohráb

Was like a maddened elephant; he struck

Rostám a blow and felled him to the earth.

830   Then like a lion in the hunt whose claws

Have thrown a mighty stallion to the ground,

Sohráb sat firmly on the chest of huge

Rostám, fist, face, and mouth all smeared with dirt,

And from his belt he drew his polished knife,

همی خواست از تن سرش را برید

بسهراب گفت ای یل شیرگیر

کمندافگن و گرد و شمشیر گیر

دگر گونه تر باشد آیین ما

جزین باشد آرایش دین ما

۸۳۵ کسی کو بکشتی نبرد آورد

سر مهتری زیر گرد آورد

نخستین که پشتش نهد برزمین

نبرّد سرش گرچه باشد بکین

گرش بار دیگر بزیر آورد

ز افگندنش نام شیر آورد

بدان چاره از چنگ آن اژدها

همی خواست کاید ز کشتن رها

دلیر جوان سر بگفتار پیر

بداد و ببود این سخن دلپذیر

۸۴۰ رها کرد زو دست و آمد بدشت

چو شیری که بر پیش آهو گذشت

همی کرد نخچیر و یادش نبود

ازان کس که بااو نبرد آزمود

همی دیرشد تا که هومان چو گرد

بیامد بپرسیدش از هم نبرد

بهومان بگفت آن کجا رفته بود

سخن هرچه رستم بدو گفته بود

بدو گفت هومان گرد ای جوان

As he bent down to sever head from trunk.

Rostám cried out, "Oh, lion-slaying chief,

And master of the sword and mace and rope!

The custom of our nation is not thus.

Our faith commands us to another way.

835 Whoever in a wrestling match first throws

His noble adversary to the ground,

And pins him to the earth, may not cut off

His head, not even if he seeks revenge.

But if he fells him twice, he's earned that right,

And all will call him Lion if he does."

By that deceit he shrewdly sought to free

Himself from this fierce dragon's mortal grip.

    The brave youth bowed his head and yielded

To the old man's words, and said no more,

840 But loosed his grip and rushed off to the plain,

A lion who has seen a deer race by.

He hunted eagerly and gave no thought

To him with whom he'd fought so recently.

When it grew late, Humán came swiftly to

The field, and asked him how the battle'd gone.

Sohráb informed Humán of all he'd done,

And what Rostám had said to him. The brave

Humán just heaved a sigh and said, "Dear youth,

بسیری رسیدی همانا ز جان

۸۴۵ دریغ این بر و بازو و یال تو

میان یلی چنگ و گوپال تو

هژبری که آورده بودی بدام

رها کردی از دام و شد کار خام

نگه کن کزین بیهده کارکرد

چه آرد بپیشت بدیگر نبرد

بگفت و دل از جان او برگرفت

پر انده همی ماند ازو در شگفت

بلشکرگه خویش بنهاد روی

بخشم و دل از غم پر از کار اوی

۸۵۰ یکی داستان زد برین شهریار

که دشمن مدار ارچه خردست خوار

چو رستم ز دست وی آزاد شد

بسان یکی تیغ پولاد شد

خرامان بشد سوی آب روان

چنان چون شده باز یابد روان

بخورد آب و روی و سر و تن بشست

بپیش جهان آفرین شد نخست

همی خواست پیروزی و دستگاه

نبود آگه از بخشش هور و ماه

۸۵۵ که چون رفت خواهد سپهر از برش

بخواهد ربودن کلاه از سرش

I see that you've grown weary of your life.

845 I fear for this stout neck and arms and chest,

This hero's waist and royal legs and feet.

You caught a tiger firm within your trap,

Then spoiled your work by letting him escape.

You'll see what consequence this foolish act

Of yours will have when next you meet to fight."

He spoke, despairing of his life. He paused

A while in grief, still wondering at his deed.

Sohráb returned toward his army's camp,

Perplexed at heart and angry with himself.

850 A shah once wisely spoke a proverb on

This point, "Despise no foe, however mean."

Rostám, when he'd escaped from his foe's hand,

Sprang up like a blade of hardened steel, and rushed

Off to a flowing stream that was nearby,

For he was like a man who'd been reborn.

He drank his fill, and when he'd washed his face

And limbs, he bowed before his Lord in prayer.

He asked for strength and victory; he did

Not know what sun and moon might hold in store,

855 Or if the heavens as they wheeled above

Would wish to snatch the crown from off his head.

وزان آبخور شد بجای نبرد

پر اندیشه بودش دل و روی زرد

همی تاخت سهراب چون پیل مست

کمندی ببازو کمانی بدست

گرازان و برگور نعره زنان

سمندش جهان و جهانرا کَنان

همی ماند رستم ازو در شگفت

ز پیگارش اندازها بَر گرفت

۸۶۰   چو سهراب شیر اوژن اورا بدید

ز باد جوانی دلش بر دمید

چنین گفت کای رسته از چنگ شیر

جدا مانده از زخم شیر دلیر

دگر باره اسپان ببستند سخت

بسر برهمی گشت بدخواه بخت

بکشتی گرفتن نهادند سر

گرفتند هردو دوال کمر

هرآنگه که خشم آورد بخت شوم

کند سنگ خارا بکردار موم

۸۶۵   سرافراز سهراب با زور دست

تو گفتی سپهر بلندش ببست

غمی بود رستم بیازید چنگ

گرفت آن بر و یال جنگی پلنگ

Then pale of face and with an anxious heart,

He left the stream to meet his foe once more.

While like a maddened elephant, Sohráb

With bow and lasso galloped on the plain.

He wheeled and shouted as he chased his prey;

His yellow steed leaped high and tore the earth.

Rostám could not but stand in awe of him;

He sought to take his measure for the fight.

860 And when the lion-slayer saw him there,

The arrogance of youth boiled up in him.

"Hail him who fled the lion's claws,

And kept himself apart from his fierce blows."

§ *The Death of Sohráb*

Again they firmly hitched their steeds, as ill-

Intentioned fate revolved above their heads.

Once more they grappled hand to hand. Each seized

The other's belt and sought to throw him down.

Whenever evil fortune shows its wrath,

It makes a block of granite soft as wax.

865 Sohráb had mighty arms, and yet it seemed

The skies above had bound them fast. He paused

In fear; Rostám stretched out his hands and seized

That warlike leopard by his chest and arms.

خم آورد پشت دلیر جوان

زمانه بیامد نبودش توان

زدش برزمین بر بکردار شیر

بدانست کو هم نماند بزیر

سبک تیغ تیز از میان بر کشید

بر شیر بیدار دل بردرید

۸۷۰ بپیچید زانپس یکی آه کرد

ز نیک و بد اندیشه کوتاه کرد

بدو گفت کین بر من از من رسید

زمانه بدست تو دادم کلید

تو زین بیگناهی که این کوژپشت

مرا برکشید و بزودی بکشت

ببازی بکویند هم سال من

بخاک اندر آمد چنین یال من

نشان داد مادر مرا از پدر

ز مهر اندر آمد روانم بسر

۸۷۵ هر آنگه که تشنه شدستی بخون

بیالودی آن خنجر آبگون

زمانه بخون تو تشنه شود

بر اندام تو موی دشنه شود

کنون گر تو در آب ماهی شوی

وگر چون شب اندر سیاهی شوی

وگر چون ستاره شوی بر سپهر

ببرّی ز روی زمین پاک مهر

He bent his strong and youthful back, and with

A lion's speed, he threw him to the ground.

Sohráb had not the strength; his time had come.

Rostám was sure he'd not stay down for long.

He swiftly drew a dagger from his belt

And tore the breast of that stout-hearted youth.

870   He writhed upon the ground; groaned once aloud,

Then thought no more of good and ill. He told

Rostám, "This was the fate allotted me.

The heavens gave my key into your hand.

It's not your fault. It was this hunchback fate,

Who raised me up then quickly cast me down.

While boys my age still spent their time in games,

My neck and shoulders stretched up to the clouds.

My mother told me who my father was.

My love for him has ended in my death.

875   Whenever you should thirst for someone's blood,

And stain your silver dagger with his gore,

Then Fate may thirst for yours as well, and make

Each hair upon your trunk a sharpened blade.

Now should you, fishlike, plunge into the sea,

Or cloak yourself in darkness like the night,

Or like a star take refuge in the sky,

And sever from the earth your shining light,

بخواهد هم ازتو پدر کین من

چو بیند که خاکست بالین من

۸۸۰ ازین نامداران گردنکشان

کسی هم بَرَد سوی رستم نشان

که سهراب کشتست و افگنده خوار

ترا خواست کردن همی خواستار

چو بشنید رستم سرش خیره گشت

جهان پیش چشم اندرش تیره گشت

بپرسید زان پس که آمد بهوش

بدو گفت با ناله و باخروش

که اکنون چه داری ز رستم نشان

که کم باد نامش ز گردنکشان

۸۸۵ بدو گفت ار ایدونکه رستم تویی

بکشتی مرا خیره از بدخویی

ز هر گونهٔ بودمت رهنمای

نجنبید یک ذرّه مِهرت ز جای

چو برخاست آواز کوس از درم

بیامد پر از خون دو رخ مادرم

همی جانش از رفتن من بخست

یکی مهره بر بازوی من ببست

مرا گفت کین از پدر یادگار

بدار و ببین تاکی آید بکار

۸۹۰ کنون کارگر شد که بیکار گشت

پسر پیش چشم پدرخوار گشت

Still when he learns that earth's my pillow now,

My father will avenge my death on you.

880   A hero from among this noble band

Will take this seal and show it to Rostám.

'Sohráb's been slain, and humbled to the earth,'

He'll say, 'This happened while he searched for you.'"

When he heard this, Rostám was near to fainting.

The world around grew dark before his eyes.

And when Rostám regained his wits once more,

He asked Sohráb with sighs of grief and pain,

"What sign have you from him—Rostám? Oh, may

His name be lost to proud and noble men!"

885   "If you're Rostám," he said, "you slew me while

Some evil humor had confused your mind."

I tried in every way to draw you forth,

But not an atom of your love was stirred.

When first they beat the war drums at my door,

My mother came to me with bloody cheeks.[31]

Her soul was racked by grief to see me go.

She bound a seal upon my arm, and said

'This is your father's gift, preserve it well.

A day will come when it will be of use.'

890   Alas, its day has come when mine has passed.

The son's abased before his father's eyes.

همان نیز مادر بروشن روان

فرستاد بامن یکی پهلوان

کجا نام آن نامور ژند بود

زبان و روان از در پند بود

بدان تا پدر را نماید بمن

سخن بر گشاید بهر انجمن

چو آن نامور پهلوان کشته شد

مرا نیز هم روز برگشته شد

۸۹۵ کنون بند بگشای از جوشنم

برهنه نگه کن تن روشنم

چو بگشاد خفتان و آن مهره دید

همه جامه بر خویشتن بر درید

همی گفت کای کشته بردست من

دلیر و ستوده بهر انجمن

همی ریخت خون و همی کند موی

سرش پر ز خاک و پراز آب روی

بدو گفت سهراب کین بدتریست

بآب دو دیده نباید گریست

۹۰۰ ازین خویشتن کشتن اکنون چه سود

چنین رفت و این بودنی کار بود

چو خورشید تابان ز گنبد بگشت

تهمتن نیامد بلشکر زدشت

ز لشکر بیامد هشیوار بیست

که تا اندر آوردگه کار چیست

My mother with great wisdom thought to send

With me a worthy *pahlaván* as guide.

The noble warrior's name was Zhende Razm,

A man both wise in action and in speech.

He was to point my father out to me,

And ask for him in every gathering,

But Zhende Razm, that worthy man, was slain.

And at his death my star declined as well.

895 Now loose the binding of my coat of mail,

And look upon my naked, shining flesh."

When Rostám undid his armor's ties, and saw

That seal, he tore his clothes and wept.

"Oh, brave and noble youth, and praised among

All men, whom I have slain with my own hand! "

He wept a bloody stream and tore his hair;

His brow was dark with dust, tears filled his eyes.

Sohráb admonished him, "But this is worse.

You must not fill your eyes with tears. It does

900 No good to slay yourself with grief. Not now.

What's happened here is what was meant to be."

When the radiant sun had left the sky,

And Tahamtán had not returned to camp,

Some twenty cavaliers rode off to see

How matters stood upon the field of war.

دو اسپ اندر آن دشت برپای بود

پر از گرد رستم دگر جای بود

گو پیلتن را چو بر پشت زین

ندیدند گردان بران دشت کین

۹۰۵ گمانشان چنان بد که او کشته شد

سر نامداران همه گشته شد

بکاؤس کی تاختند آگهی

که تخت مهی شد ز رستم تهی

ز لشکر برآمد سراسر خروش

زمانه یکایک برآمد بجوش

بفرمود کاؤس تا بوق و کوس

دمیدند و آمد سپهدار طوس

ازان پس بدو گفت کاؤس شاه

کز ایدر هیونی سوی رزمگاه

۹۱۰ بتازید تا کار سهراب چیست

که بر شهر ایران بباید گریست

اگر کشته شد رستم جنگجوی

از ایران که یارد شدن پیش اوی

بانبوه زخمی بباید زدن

برین رزمگه برنشاید بُدن

چو آشوب برخاست از انجمن

چنین گفت سهراب با پیلتن

که اکنون که روز من اندر گذشت

همه کار ترکان دگر گونه گشت

They saw two horses standing on the plain,

Both caked with dirt. Rostám was somewhere else.

Because they did not see his massive form

Upon the battlefield and mounted on

905   His steed, the heroes thought that he'd been slain.

The nobles all grew fearful and perplexed.

They sent a mesage swiftly to the shah,

"The throne of majesty has lost Rostám."

From end to end the army cried aloud,

And suddenly confusion filled the air.

Kavús commanded that the horns and drums

Be sounded, and his marshal, Tus, approached.

Then Kavus spoke, "Be quick, and gallop your horse

From here to view the battlefield,

910   And see how matters stand with bold Sohráb.

Must we lament the passing of Irán?

If by his hand the brave Rostám's been slain,

Who from Irán will dare approach this foe?

We must plan to strike a wide and general blow;

We dare not tarry long upon this field."

And while a tumult rose within their camp,

Sohráb was speaking with brave Tahamtán,

"The situation of the Turks has changed

In every way now that my days are done.

۹۱۵ همه مهربانی بران کن که شاه

سوی جنگ ترکان نراند سپاه

که ایشان ز بهر مرا جنگجوی

سوی مرز ایران نهادند روی

بسی روز را داده بودم نوید

بسی کرده بودم زهر در امید

نباید که بینند رنجی براه

مکن جز بنیکی بر ایشان نگاه

نشست از بر رخش رستم چو گَرد

پراز خون رخ و لب پراز باد سرد

۹۲۰ بیامد بپیش سپه با خروش

دل از کردهٔ خویش با درد و جوش

چو دیدند ایرانیان روی اوی

همه برنهادند برخاک روی

ستایش گرفتند برکردگار

که او زنده باز آمد از کارزار

چو زان گونه دیدند برخاک سر

دریده برو جامه و خسته بر

بپرسش گرفتند کین کار چیست

ترا دل برین گونه از بهر کیست

۹۲۵ بگفت آن شگفتی که خود کرده بود

گرامی تر خود بیازرده بود

همه بر گرفتند با او خروش

زمین پر خروش و هوا پر ز جوش

915 Be kind to them, and do not let the shah

Pursue this war or urge his army on.

It was for me the Turkish troops rose up,

And mounted this campaign against Irán.

I it was who promised victory, and I

Who strove in every way to give them hope.

They should not suffer now as they retreat.

Be generous with them, and let them go."

Rostám swiftly mounted Rakhsh, but as he did,

His eyes bled tears, his lips were chilled with sighs.

920 He wept as he approached the army's camp,

His heart was filled with pain at what he'd done.

When they first spied his face, the army of Irán

Fell prostrate to the earth in gratitude,

And loudly praised the Maker of the World,

That he'd returned alive and well from war.

But when they saw him with chest and clothes

All torn, his body heavy and his face

Begrimed by dust, they asked him with one voice,

"What does this mean? Why are you sad at heart?"

925 He told them of his strange and baffling deed,

Of how he'd slain the one he held most dear.

They all began to weep and mourn with him,

And filled the earth and sky with loud lament.

چنین گفت با سرفرازان که من

نه دل دارم امروز گویی نه تن

شما جنگ ترکان مجویید کس

همین بد که من کردم امروز بس

چو برگشت ازان جایگه پهلوان

بیامد بر پور خسته روان

۹۳۰　بزرگان برفتند بااو بهم

چو طوس و چو گودرز و چون گستهم

همه لشکر از بهر آن ارجمند

زبان برگشادند یکسر ز بند

که درمان این کار یزدان کند

مگر کین سخن برتو آسان کند

یکی دشنه بگرفت رستم بدست

که از تن ببرّد سر خویش پست

بزرگان بدو اندر آویختند

ز مژگان همی خون فرو ریختند

۹۳۵　بدو گفت گودرز کاکنون چه سود

که از روی گیتی برآری تو دود

تو برخویشتن گر کنی صد گزند

چه آسانی آید بدان ارجمند

اگر ماند او را بگیتی زمان

بماند تو بی رنج بااو بمان

وگر زین جهان این جوان رفتنیست

بگیتی نگه کن که جاوید کیست

At last he told the nobles gathered there,

"It seems my heart is gone, my body too.

Do not pursue this battle with the Turks.

The evil I have done is quite enough."

And when he left that place, the *pahlaván*

Returned with weary heart to where he lay.

930 The noble lords accompanied their chief,

Men like Gudárz and Tus and Gostahám.

The army all together loosed their tongues,

And gave advice and counsel to Rostám,

"Yazdán alone can remedy this wound;

He yet may ease this burden's weight for you."

He grasped a dagger in his hand, and made

To cut his worthless head from his own trunk.

The nobles hung upon his arm and hand,

And tears of blood poured from their eyes.

935 Gudárz said to Rostám, "What gain is there

If by your death you set the world aflame?[32]

Were you to give yourself a hundred wounds,

How would that ease the pain of brave Sohráb?

If some time yet remains for him on earth,

He'll live, and you'll remain with him, at peace.

But if this youth is destined to depart,

Look on the world, who's there that does not die?

شکاریم یکسر همه پیش مرگ

سری زیر تاج وسری زیر ترگ

۹۴۰　بگودرز گفت آنزمان پهلوان

کز ایدر برو زود روشن روان

پیامی ز من پیش کاؤس بر

بگویش که ما را چه آمد بسر

بدشنه جگرگاه پور دلیر

دریدم که رستم مماناد دیر

گرت هیچ یادست کردار من

یکی رنجه کن دل بتیمار من

ازان نوشدارو که در گنج تست

کجا خستگان را کند تن درست

۹۴۵　بنزدیک من بایکی جام می

سزد گر فرستی هم اکنون بپی

مگر کو ببخت تو بهتر شود

چو من پیش تخت تو کهتر شود

بیامد سپهبد بکردار باد

بکاؤس یکسر پیامش بداد

بدو گفت کاؤس کز انجمن

اگر زنده ماند چنان پیل تن

شود پشت رستم بنیرو ترا

هلاک آورد بی گمانی مرا

The head that wears a helmet and the head

That wears a crown, to death we all are prey."

§*Rostám Asks Kay Kavús for the Nushdarú*

940 Rostám called wise Gudárz and said to him,

"Depart from here upon your swiftest steed,

And take a message to Kavús the shah.

Tell him what has befallen me. With my

Own dagger I have torn the breast of my

Brave son—oh, may Rostám not live for long!

If you've some recollection of my deeds,

Then share with me a portion of my grief,

And from your store send me the *nushdarú*,

That medicine which heals whatever wound.

945 It would be well if you sent it to me

With no delay, and in a cup of wine.

By your good grace, my son may yet be cured,

And like his father stand before your throne."

The *sepahbód* Gudárz rode like the wind,

And gave Kavús the message from Rostám.

Kavús replied, "If such an elephant

Should stay alive and join our royal court,

He'll make his father yet more powerful.

Rostám will slay me then, I have no doubt.

۹۵۰ اگر یک زمان زو بمن بد رسد

نسازیم پاداش او جز به بد

کجا گنجد او درجهان فراخ

بدان فرّ و آن برز و آن یال وشاخ

شنیدی که او گفت کاؤس کیست

گر او شهریارست پس طوس کیست

کجا باشد او پیش تختم بپای

کجا راند او زیر فرّ همای

چو بشنید گودرز برگشت زود

بر رستم آمد بکردار دود

۹۵۵ بدو گفت خوی بد شهریار

درختیست جنگی همیشه ببار

ترا رفت باید بنزدیک او

درفشان کنی جان تاریک او

بفرمود رستم که تا پیشکار

یکی جامه افگند بر جویبار

جوانرا بران جامه آنجایگاه

بخوابید و آمد بنزدیک شاه

گوپیلتن سر سوی راه کرد

کس آمد پیش زود و آگاه کرد

۹۶۰ که سهراب شد زین جهان فراخ

همی از تو تابوت خواهد نه کاخ

950 When I may suffer evil at his hands,

What gift but evil should I make him now?

You heard him, how he said, 'Who is Kavús?

If he's the shah, then who is Tus?' And with

That chest and neck, that mighty arm and fist,

In this wide world, who's there to equal him?

Will he stand humbly by my royal seat,

Or march beneath my banner's eagle wings?"

Gudárz heard his reply, then turned and rode

Back to Rostám as swift as wind-borne smoke.

955 "The evil nature of the shah is like

The tree of war, perpetually in fruit.

You must depart at once and go to him.

Perhaps you can enlighten his dark soul."

§*Rostám Mourns Sohráb*

Rostám commanded that a servant bring

A robe and spread it by the river's bank.

He gently laid Sohráb upon the robe,

Then mounted Rakhsh and rode toward the shah.

But as he rode, his face toward the court,

They overtook him swiftly with the news,

960 "Sohráb has passed from this wide world; he'll need

A coffin from you now, and not a crown.

پدر جست و برزد یکی سردباد

بنالید و مژگان بهم برنهاد

پیاده شد از اسپ رستم چوباد

بجای گُله خاک برسر نهاد

همی گفت زار ای نبرده جوان

سرافراز و از تخمهٔ پهلوان

نبیند چو تو نیز خورشید و ماه

نه جوشن نه تخت و نه تاج و کلاه

۹۶۵   کرا آمد این پیش کامد مرا

بکشتم جوانی بپیران سرا

نبیره جهاندار سام سوار

سوی مادر از تخمهٔ نامدار

بریدن دو دستم سزاوار هست

جز از خاک تیره مبادم نشست

کدامین پدر هرگز این کار کرد

سزاوارم اکنون بگفتار سرد

بگیتی که کشتست فرزند را

دلیر و جوان و خردمند را

۹۷۰   نکوهش فراوان کند زال زر

همان نیز رودابهٔ پرهنر

بدین کار پوزش چه پیش آورم

که دل شان بگفتار خویش آورم

چه گویند گردان و گردنکشان

چو زین سان شود نزد ایشان نشان

'Father! ' he cried, then sighed an icy wind,

Then wept aloud and closed his eyes at last."

    Rostám dismounted from his steed at once.

Dark dust replaced the helmet on his head.

He wept and cried aloud, "Oh, noble youth,

And proud, courageous seed of *pahlaváns*!

The sun and moon won't see your like again,

No more will shield or mail, nor throne or crown.

965 Who else has been afflicted as I've been?

That I should slay a youth in my old age

Who is descended from world-conquering Sam,

Whose mother's seed's from famous men as well.

It would be right to sever these two hands.

No seat be mine henceforth save darkest earth.

What father's ever done a deed like this?

I deserve abuse and icy scorn, no more.

Who else in all this world has slain his son,

His wise, courageous, youthful son?

970 How Zal the golden will rebuke me now,

He and the virtuous Rudabé as well.

What can I offer them as my excuse?

What plea of mine will satisfy their hearts?

What will the heroes and the warriors say

When word of this is carried to their ears?

چه گویم چو آگه شود مادرش

چه گونه فرستم کسیرا برش

چه گویم چرا کشتمش بی گناه

چرا روز کردم برو برسیاه

۹۷۵   پدرش آن گرانمایهٔ پهلوان

چه گوید بدان پاک دخت جوان

برین تخمهٔ سام نفرین کنند

همه نام من نیز بی دین کنند

که دانست کین کودک ارجمند

بدین سال گردد چو سرو بلند

بجنگ آیدش رای و سازد سپاه

بمن بر کند روز روشن سیاه

بفرمود تا دیبهٔ خسروان

کشیدند بر روی پور جوان

۹۸۰   همی آرزوگاه و شهر آمدش

یکی تنگ تابوت بهر آمدش

ازان دشت بردند تابوت اوی

سوی خیمهٔ خویش بنهاد روی

بپرده سرای آتش اندر زدند

همه لشکرش خاک برسر زدند

همان خیمه و دیبه هفت رنگ

همه تخت پرمایه زرین پلنگ

برآتش نهادند و برخاست غو

And when his mother learns, what shall I say?

How can I send a messenger to her?

What shall I say? Why did I slay him when

He'd done no crime? Why blacken all his days?

975 How will her father, that worthy *pahlaván*,

Report this to his pure and youthful child?

He'll call this seed of Sam a godless wretch,

And heap his curses on my name and line.

Alas, who could have known this precious child

Would quickly grow to cypress height, or that

He'd raise this host and think of arms and war,

Or that he'd turn my shining day to night."

    Rostám commanded that the body of

His son be covered with a royal robe.

980 He'd longed to sit upon the throne and rule;

His portion was a coffin's narrow walls.

The coffin of Sohráb was carried from

The field. Rostám returned to his own tent.

They set aflame Sohráb's pavilion while

His army cast dark dust upon their heads.

They threw his tents of many colored silk,

His precious throne and leopard saddle cloth

Into the flames, and tumult filled the air.

همی گفت زار ای جهاندار نو

۹۸۵   دریغ آن رخ و برز و بالای تو

دریغ آن همه مردی و رای تو

دریغ این غم و حسرت جان گسل

ز مادر جدا وز پدر داغ دل

همی ریخت خون و همی کند خاک

همه جامهٔ خسروی کرد چاک

همه پهلوانان کاوس شاه

نشستند برخاک با او براه

زبان بزرگان پراز پند بود

تهمتن بدرد از جگر بند بود

۹۹۰   چنین ست کردار چرخ بلند

بدستی کلاه و بدیگر کمند

چو شادان نشیند کسی با کلاه

بخمّ کمندش رباید ز گاه

چرا مهر باید همی بر جهان

چو باید خرامید با همرهان

چو اندیشهٔ گنج گردد دراز

همی گشت باید سوی خاک باز

اگر چرخ را هست ازین آگهی

همانا که گشتست مغزش تهی

۹۹۵   چنان دان کزین گردش آگاه نیست

که چون و چرا سوی او راه نیست

Rostam lamented, "Oh, youthful conqueror!

985 Alas, that stature and that noble face!

Alas, that wisdom and that manliness!

Alas, what sorrow and heart-rending loss—

Mother far off, slain by his father's hand."

His eyes wept bloody tears, he tore the earth,

And rent the kingly garments on his back.

Then all the *pahlaváns* and Shah Kavús

Sat with him in the dust beside the road.

They spoke to him with counsel and advice—

In grief Rostám was like one driven mad—

990 "This is the way of fortune's wheel. It holds

A lasso in this hand, a crown in that.

As one sits happily upon his throne,

A loop of rope will snatch him from his place.

Why is it we should hold the world so dear?

We and our fellows must soon travel on.

The longer we have thought about our wealth,

The sooner we must face that earthy door.

If heaven's wheel knows anything of this,

Or if its mind is empty of our fate,

995 The turning of the wheel it cannot know,

Nor can it understand the reason why.

بدین رفتن اکنون نباید گریست

ندانم که کارش بفرجام چیست

برستم چنین گفت کاؤس کی

که از کوه البرز تا برگ نی

همی برد خواهد بگردش سپهر

نباید فگندن بدین خاک مهر

یکی زود سازد یکی دیرتر

سرانجام بر مرگ باشد گذر

۱۰۰۰ تو دلرا بدین رفته خرسند کن

همه گوش سوی خردمند کن

اگر آسمان برزمین برزنی

وگر آتش اندر جهان در زنی

نیابی همان رفته را باز جای

روانش کهن شد بدیگر سرای

من از دور دیدم بر و یال اوی

چنان برز وبالا وگو پال اوی

زمانه برانگیختش با سپاه

که ایدر بدست تو گردد تباه

۱۰۰۵ چه سازی ودرمان این کار چیست

برین رفته تاچند خواهی گریست

بدو گفت رستم که او خود گذشت

نشست هومان درین پهن دشت

ز توران سرانند و چندی ز چین

ازیشان بدل در مدار ایچ کین

One must lament that he should leave this world,

Yet what this means at last, I do not know."

   Then Kay Kavús spoke to Rostám at length,

"From Mount Alborz down to the frailest reed,

The turning heavens carry all away.

You must not fix your heart upon this world.

One sets off quickly on the road, and one

Will take more time, but all pass on to death.

1000   Content your heart with his departure and

Give careful heed to what I tell you now.

If you should bring the heavens down to earth,

Or set the world aflame from end to end,

You won't recall from death the one who's gone.

His soul's grown ancient in that other dwelling.

Once from afar I saw his arms and neck,

His lofty stature and his massive chest.

The times impelled him and his martial host

To come here now and perish by your hand.

1005   What can you do? What remedy is there

For death? For how long can you mourn and weep?"

   Rostám replied, "Though he himself is gone,

Humán still sits upon this ample plain,

His Turkish and his Chinese chiefs as well.

Retain no hint of enmity toward them,

زواره سپه را گذارد براه

بنیروی یزدان و فرمان شاه

بدو گفت شاه ای گو نامجوی

ازین رزم اندوهت آید بروی

۱۰۱۰ گر ایشان بمن چند بدکرده اند

وگر دود از ایران برآورده اند

دل من ز درد تو شد پر ز درد

نخواهم از ایشان همی یادکرد

بفرمود کاووس خورشید فر

که باشد زواره بدین راهبر

زواره بیامد برآن انجمن

دریده همه جامهٔ خویشتن

فرستاد نزدیک هومان پیام

که شمشیر کین ماند اندر نیام

۱۰۱۵ نگهبان این لشکر اکنون توی

نگه کن بدیشان نگر نغنوی

وز انجایگه شاه لشکر براند

به ایران خرامید و رستم بماند

بدان تا زواره بیاید ز راه

بدو آگهی آورد زان سپاه

چو آمد زواره سپیده دمان

سپه راند رستم هم اندر زمان

پس آنگه سوی زابلستان کشید

But strengthened by Yazdán and your command,

Let Zavaré guide all their army home."

"Oh, famous *pahlaván*," said Shah Kavús,

This war has caused you suffering and loss.

1010   Though they have done me many grievous wrongs,

And though Turán has set Irán aflame,

Because my heart can feel your heavy pain,

I'll think no more of them and let them go."[33]

§*Rostám Conveys His Son to Zabolestán*

Kavús, whose radiance outshone the sun,

Commanded that his brother stay as guide.

Then Zavaré approached the royal throng,

The clothes upon his body torn to shreds.

He sent a message to Humán which said,

The sword of vengeance stays within its sheath.

1015   *You are commander of this army now,*

Observe their conduct well, and do not sleep.

The shah departed from the field and led

His army to Irán, Rostám remained

To wait until brave Zavaré returned,

And brought him news of how that army'd fared.

When Zavaré returned at break of day,

Rostam commanded that the troops form ranks

At once, then led them toward Zabolestan.

چو آگاهی از وی بدستان رسید

۱۰۲۰ همه سیستان پیش بازآمدند

برنج و بدرد و گداز آمدند

چو تابوت را دید دستان سام

فرود آمد از اسپ زرّین ستام

تهمتن پیاده همی رفت پیش

دریده همه جامه دل کرده ریش

گشادند گردان سراسر کمر

همه پیش تابوت برخاک سر

همی گفت زال اینت کاری شگفت

که سهراب گرز گران برگرفت

۱۰۲۵ نشانی شد اندر میان مهان

نزاید چنو مادر اندر جهان

همی گفت و مژگان پراز آب کرد

زبان پر ز گفتار سهراب کرد

چو آمد تهمتن به ایوان خویش

خروشید و تابوت بنهاد پیش

ازو میخ بر کند و بگشاد سر

کفن زو جدا کرد پیش پدر

تنش را بدان نامداران نمود

تو گفتی که از چرخ بر خاست دود

۱۰۳۰ مهان جهان جامه کردند چاک

به ابر اندر آمد سر گرد و خاک

همه کاخ تابوت بد سربسر

When news of their arrival reached Dastán,

1020 All in Sistán went forth to meet Rostám;

They came to him prostrate with pain and grief.

When first he looked upon that wooden bier,

Dastán dismounted from his golden saddle.

Rostám came forward then, on foot. His clothes

Were torn to shreds, his heart was pierced by grief.

The heroes one and all let fall their arms,

And bowed down to the earth before his bier.

Zal spoke, "This was a strange event indeed.

Sohráb could lift the heavy mace; of this

1025 The greatest in the land would speak with awe.

No mother in the world will bear his like."

And Zal spoke on; his eyes were filled with tears

His tongue with words of praise for bold Sohráb.

When Tahamtán had reached his palace gate,

He cried aloud and set the coffin down.

He wrenched the nails out, threw the lid aside,

And drew the shroud off as his father watched,

Showing his son's body to those noble men.

It was as if the heavens burned with grief.

1030 Those famous heroes tore their clothes and wept;

Like dust their cries ascended to the clouds.

From end to end the palace seemed a tomb,

غنوده بصندوق در شیر نر

تو گفتی که سام است بایال و سفت

غمی شد ز جنگ اندر آمد بخفت

بپوشید بازش بدیبای زرد

سرتنگ تابوت را سخت کرد

همی گفت اگر دخمه زرّین کنم

ز مشک سیه گردش آگین کنم

۱۰۳۵　چو من رفته باشم نماند بجای

وگرنه مرا خود جزین نیست رای

یکی دخمه کردش ز سمّ ستور

جهانی ز زاری همی گشت کور

چنین گفت بهرام نیکو سخن

که با مردگان آشنایی مکن

نه ایدر همی ماند خواهی دراز

بسیچیده باش و درنگی مساز

بتو داد یکروز نوبت پدر

سزد گرترا نوبت آید بسر

۱۰۴۰　چنین است و رازش نیامد پدید

نیابی بخیره چه جویی کلید

در بسته را کس نداند گشاد

بدین رنج عمر تو گردد بباد

یکی داستانست پرآب چشم

دل نازک از رستم آید بخشم

In which a lion had been laid to rest.

It seemed as though great Sam was lying there.

The battle'd wearied him, and now he slept.

He covered him again with gold brocade,

And firmly closed the coffin's narrow lid.

"If now I build Sohráb a golden tomb

And strew it round with fragrant, sable musk,

1035   When I am gone, it won't remain for long.

If that's not so, yet so it seems to me."

With horses' hooves they built a warrior's tomb,

And all the world went blind with weeping there.

Thus spoke Bahrám the wise and eloquent,

"Don't bind yourself too closely to the dead,

For you yourself will not remain here long.

Prepare yourself to leave, and don't be slow.

One day your sire gave you a turn at life.

The turn is at its end, that's only right.

1040   That's how it is, the secret why's unknown.

The door is locked; nor will the key be found.

You won't discover it, don't even try!

And if you do, you'll spend your life in vain."

It is a tale that's filled with tears and grief.

The tender heart will rage against Rostám.

Notes

Introduction

1. The relation of Ferdowsi to the Iranian national epic tradition has been reviewed most recently and authoritatively by Olga M. Davidson in "The Crown-Bestower in the Iranian Book of Kings," *Studia Iranica*, vol. 10, Papers in Honor of Professor Mary Boyce (Leiden: E. J. Brill, 1985), see particularly pt. 2: "The Authority and Authenticity of Ferdowsi's Book of Kings." The development of the epic tradition after Ferdowsi's completion of his work is reviewed in various places, most recently and best in William L. Hanaway, "The Iranian Epics" in *Heroic Epic and Saga*, ed. Felix J. Oinas (Bloomington: University of Indiana Press, 1978).

2. All references to the text are to the edition prepared by Ye. E. Bertel's et al., eds., *Shāh-nāme*, 9 vols. (Moscow: AN SSSR, 1960–71). This abbreviation means volume 3, page 6, line 9. All translations are my own.

Translation

1. The terms *dehqán* and *mobád* refer to the Iranian provincial nobility of Central Asia and to Zoroastrian clerics, respectively. These are the two classes who are identified in the

Shahname as the principal repositories of the pre-Islamic Iranian culture of which it is a part.'

2. Onagers (*equus onager*) are a species of wild ass native to the Iranian plateau and Central Asia.

3. This epithet for Rostám refers to his role in bringing Kay Qobád to the throne, thus forestalling the ascension of Afrasiyáb. Kay Qobád was the first shah of the Kaianian dynasty and Kay Kavús was his successor. The incident of Rostám and Kay Qobád is told in the account of the reign of Garshásp.

4. Rostám's steed, Rakhsh, is as hugely proportioned as he is himself, and the only horse able to bear his weight. He is also his companion in all his adventures and sometimes takes an active role in them. During the series of adventures that heralds Rostám's entry into the epic as its paramount hero, Rakhsh finds a spring during their journey across the desert, and later warns Rostám of a dragon's approach.

5. The epithet Tahamtán, which means "huge-bodied," is commonly used for Rostám.

6. The round face and pale skin of the moon are the type of feminine beauty in Persian poetry.

7. Izád is one of the names of God.

8. In the margin of the Florence manuscript, and in a later hand, several couplets have been added at this point in which Rostám calls for a *mobád* to ask for Tahminé's hand from her father and to bless their marriage. This despite the reference in the next line to the secrecy of the union. These couplets appear in the text of the British Museum manuscript, and in all subsequent manuscripts, as well, often with further embellishments to the ceremony. However, they are not rendered in the Arabic translation of Bondari that is contemporary with the Florence manuscript. Mojtaba Minavi, who died before the Florence manuscript came to light, was of the opinion that these lines had been added by later Muslim scribes who were embarrassed by the barbarian irregularity of this union (*Dastan-i rustam va suhrab az shahnamah*, ed.

Mojtaba Minavi [Tehran: Bunyad-e Shahnamah-yi Firdawsi, 1352/1974], see the introduction and note to lines 89–92).

9. Rostám here refers to his ancestors. His was from a line of heroes famed for generations. The likeness of Sohráb to his grandfather, Sam, is remarked on repeatedly in the course of the poem.

10. That is, because his face flushed red when he laughed, she called him by a name that means rosy hued. In Persian, red is the color of health and good cheer. Rostám's face flushes red with pleasure when he sees the plain filled with game, for example. Yellow by contrast is the color of fear and ill-health.

11. I take this reading from the Florence manuscript. Other manuscripts have lines that indicate either that Sohráb is a fierce tiger who reveals his lineage in his prowess (Minavi, *Dastan*, p. 33, l. 142), or that proven worth is superior to Sohráb's promise (Bertel's, *Shāh-nāme*, vol. 2, p. 180, l. 147). Since Afrasiyáb seems to assume in his response to this report that he is confident Sohráb will triumph over Rostám unless deflected by filial love, I have chosen the line that anticipates that sentiment.

12. The name Gordafaríd means "created a warrior."

13. The text here reads Azár Goshasp, who in Iranian mythology is an angel who lives in fire.

14. Zaból and Zabolestán are the names given to the ancient province of Iran that lies on what is now the central border region of Iran and Afghanistan. Rostám's family are the hereditary rulers of this region.

15. Shah Kay Kavús here flatters Rostám by alluding to the famous occasions when Rostám singlehandedly rescued him and his army from defeat and ignominious captivity—first at the hands of the demon army of Mazandarán, and second at those of the rebellious monarch of Hamavarán. Rostám's magnificent victory over the demons of Mazandarán, and the heroic journey through the desert that divided Zaból from Mazandarán, which preceded it, marked his entry into the royal court of Iran as its chief hero and the successor in that office to his father and grandfather.

16. Nahíd is the Iranian name for Venus, both the planet and goddess.
17. The father of Rostám is referred to variously as Zal and Dastán.
18. The epithet Piltán means "elephant body"; like "Tahamtán" it emphasizes Rostám's enormous size.
19. See note 3 above for the story of how Rostám acquired the epithet Giver of the Crown.
20. That is, I will leave here as swiftly as I can, and not return. For this puzzling phrase, I am following the interpretation by Ja'far She'ar and Hasan Anvari, *Ghamname-ye rostam va sohrab* (Tehran: Nashr-i Nashir, 1363/1984), p. 107, l. 387n. They point out that the feathers of the vulture (*kargas*) were prized because they were believed to add speed and height to an arrow's flight.
21. The term *sepahbód* in this line and *sepahdár* in line 389 may both be translated as "leader of the army," and both terms may be applied to chiefs like Rostám and Tus as well as to Shah Kay Kavús.
22. Yazdán is one of the names of God.
23. Kavé is the blacksmith who led the Iranian people in revolt against the Arab tyrant, Zahhak. The banner he raised was his blacksmith's apron, fixed to the point of his spear. This apron, richly adorned with gold and gems and precious brocades, became the royal banner of Iran's shahs.
24. The prince newly arrived from China is, of course, Rostám, whose identity is revealed by his great height, and that of his horse, as well as by his dragon banner. The presence of the royal banner of Iran's shahs is further evidence that this is the camp of Iran's principal hero.
25. That is, on his father's side Giv is a member of the noble house of Keshvád; through his marriage to Rostám's daughter, Banugashasp, he is allied with the noble line of Rostám as well (She'ar and Anvari, *Ghamname*, p. 126, l. 566n).
26. I prefer this reading, which occurs in the Florence manuscript among others, because it provides Faribórz with a heraldic

device like that of the other heroes. The British Museum
manuscript simply has more soldiers standing at the ready.

27. Ahrimán is the name given to the God of Darkness in Iranian
    mythology.

28. Rostám's battle with the White Demon (Div Sepíd) occurs
    early in the reign of Kay Kavús. Kavús has foolishly made
    war on the kingdom of Mazandarán, where he is defeated and
    imprisoned, along with the Iranian army, by Div Sepíd and
    his demon troops. Rostám rescues them all, singlehandedly,
    in his debut as the greatest of Iran's pahlaváns.

29. This line appears in the Florence manuscript but not in the
    British Museum manuscript.

30. In Zoroastrian practice, the dead are exposed in walled enclo-
    sures until their skeletons have been picked clean by vultures.
    The bones are then collected and placed in an ossuary. In
    this way neither earth nor water is defiled by the dead.

31. Intense grief is indicated in Persian poetry by bloody tears.

32. Gudárz here gives a vivid image of the warfare and chaos
    that would result from Rostám's death. With Rostám gone
    Afrasiyáb would renew the battle for succession that devas-
    tated both countries for many years before the accession of
    Kay Qobád and the emergence of Rostám as Iran's hero.

33. The next eight lines are illegible in the British Museum
    manuscript, and I have added them from the Minavi edition.

Glossary

In the following transcription (a) represents the a of "cat," and (a̱) the a of "calm."

Afra̱siya̱b: the shah of Turán and implacable enemy of Iran whose throne he briefly held.

Ahrimán: the Iranian God of Darkness and enemy of Yazdán.

A̱zár Gosha̱sp: the Iranian angel who lives in fire.

Bahrám: son of Gudárz and brother of Giv.

Barma̱n: one of the warriors Afrasiyáb sends with Sohráb to prevent his recognizing his father.

Dasta̱n: Rostám's father, also known as Zal.

dehqa̱n: a member of the Iranian landed provincial nobility. Ferdowsi credits them in the *Shahname* with having preserved the stories and legends of the Iranian national tradition.

div: a demon that appears in the form of a monster and wars with humans.

Faribórz: the son of Kay Kavús.

Gazhdahám/Gazhdáhm: the Iranian hero who commands the White Fort.

Giv: an Iranian hero and son of Gudárz.

Gora̱zé: an Iranian hero whose name means "boar."

Gorda̱faríd: the Iranian warrior maiden who outwits Sohráb at the White Fort when she cannot outfight him. Her name

185

means "created a warrior" and she is unique within the *Shahname.*

Gorgín: an Iranian hero.

Gostahám/Gostáhm: the brother of Gordafaríd. His name is only mentioned in this tale.

Gudárz: an Iranian hero and sage counselor of the shah.

Hamavarán: a region to the west of Iran where Kay Kavús embroiled himself and his army. Rostám rescued all of them singlehandedly.

Hojír: the Iranian hero and son of Gudárz whom Sohráb defeats and takes prisoner at the White Fort. He loses his life protecting Rostám.

Humán: the Turanian general whom Afrasiyáb sends with Sohráb to aid him in his war with Iran, and prevent him from learning his father's identity.

Irán: roughly the region now occupied by Iran, Afghanistan, and western Pakistan.

Izád: one of the names of God.

Kay Kavús: the shah of Iran.

Kay Qobád: the father of Kay Kavús. He was brought to the throne by Rostám who thus earned his title of "Giver of the Crown." In his reign Afrasiyáb was driven back to Turán and the turbulence that followed the terrible reign of Shah Nowzár was ended.

Keshvád: the name of Gudárz's family—a major provincial dynasty.

Mazandarán: a region to the north of Iran. Kay Kavús was taken prisoner by an army of *divs* there. Rostám made a heroic journey through the desert to rescue them.

mobád: a priest of the Iranian religion. Used here most often simply to mean a wise man.

Nahíd: the Iranian name for Venus, both the planet and the goddess. Nahíd has the form Anahita in other Near Eastern languages.

Narimán: the great-grandfather of Rostám and the first great hero in that family's line.

nushdarú: a panacea that only the shah can dispense.

padisháh: another term for shah.

pahlaván: "hero" transformed into "paladin" in English.

Piltán: an epithet for Rostám meaning "elephant body."

Rakhsh: Rostám's horse and companion in all his adventures. Rakhsh is the only horse large enough to carry so enormous a hero.

Rohám: an Iranian hero and son of Gudárz.

Rostám: fourth in the line of royal heroes from the kindgom of Zaból and the last and greatest of them.

Rudabé: Rostám's mother.

Sam: Rostám's grandfather, who is still living in this story.

Semengán: a border province of Turán.

sepahdár/sepahbód: a title meaning general, but applied to shahs and heroes alike.

shahryár: another term for shah.

Sistán: a province to the north of Zabolestán. The region, ruled by Rostám and his ancestors, included both Sistán and Zabolestán. The two terms are used almost interchangeably in the poem to refer to his home.

Sohráb: Rostám's son by Tahminé, the daughter of the shah of Semengán.

Tahamtán/Tahmtán: an epithet for Rostám meaning "huge body."

Tahminé: the daughter of the shah of Semengán and mother of Sohráb. Her name also means "huge" although no allusion is made to her size in the story.

Taráz: a city in Central Asia famous for the beauty of its women.

Turán: the enemy of Iran whose ruler is Afrasiyáb.

Tus: an Iranian hero and son of Shah Nowzár—a cruel tyrant who was slain by Afrasiyáb. Tus is chief of the Iranian court's heroes and hostile to Rostám, but no match for him.

Yazdán: one of the names of God.

Zaból/Zabolestán: the kingdom ruled by Rostám. Modern Zabolestán is located somewhat to the south and west of the Zabolestán of the *Shahname*.

Zal: Rostám's father, also known as Dastán. The name means "ancient" and was given to him because he was born with a head of pure white hair.

Zavaré: Rostám's brother and loyal aid.

Zhende Rázm: the Turanian warrior whom Tahminé sends with Sohráb to counsel him and assure that he recognizes his father. Rostám slays him during his spying expedition to the Turanian camp.

Selected Bibliography

The only complete English translation of the *Shahname* is that of Arthur George and Edmond Warner in nine volumes entitled *The Shahnama of Firdausi* (London: Kegan Paul, 1905–25). More recently a one-volume synoptic translation by Reuben Levy was published under the title *The Epic of the Kings* by the Persian Heritage Foundation (Chicago: University of Chicago Press, 1967).

Few literary studies of the *Shahname* have appeared in English. However, there are general introductions to it in A. J. Arberry's *Classical Persian Literature* (London: Allen and Unwin, 1958), and the more scholarly *History of Iranian Literature* by Jan Rypka et al. (Holland: Dordrecht, 1968). More general background to the epic may be found in the *Cambridge History of Iran, Volume 3: The Seleucid, Parthian and Sassanian Periods*, edited by Ehsan Yarshater (New York: Cambridge University Press, 1983); contained in this volume and of particular value are the two essays by Yarshater: "Iranian Common Beliefs and World View," and "Iranian National History" (see vol. 3, pt. 3). There is also a good brief introduction to the Iranian epic tradition in William L. Hanaway, "The Iranian Epics," *Heroic Epic and Saga*, edited by Felix J. Oinas (Bloomington: University of Indiana Press, 1978).

In preparing my translation, I have followed the Moscow edition of the text by Ye. E. Bertel's et al., eds. *Shāh-nāme*, 9 vols. (Moscow: AN SSSR, 1960–71). I have consulted the text and notes of the edition of the story of Sohráb prepared by Mojtaba Minavi, *Dastan-i rustam va suhrab az shahnamah* (Tehran: Bunyad-e Shahnamah-yi Firdawsi, 1352/1974) as well, and made extensive use of the excellent and thorough annotations given by Ja'far She'ar and Hasan Anvari in their *Ghamname-ye rostam va sohrab* (Tehran: Nashr-i Nashir, 1363/1984).